BROADCASTING IN IRELAND

Other volumes in this series include

'Broadcasting in Sweden': Edward W. Ploman

'Broadcasting in Canada': E.S. Hallman
                        with H. Hindley

'Broadcasting in Peninsular Malaysia': Ronny Adhikarya
                                       with Woon Ai Leng,
                                       Wong Hock Seng,
                                       Khor Yoke Lim

'Broadcasting in the Netherlands': Kees van der Haak
                                   with Joanna Spicer

BROADCASTING IN IRELAND

Desmond Fisher

CASE STUDIES ON BROADCASTING SYSTEMS

ROUTLEDGE & KEGAN PAUL
London, Henley and Boston
in association with the
INTERNATIONAL INSTITUTE OF COMMUNICATIONS

First published in 1978
by Routledge & Kegan Paul Ltd
39 Store Street,
London WC1E 7DD,
Broadway House,
Newtown Road,
Henley-on-Thames, Oxon RG9 1EN and
9 Park Street,
Boston, Mass. 02108, USA
Printed and bound in Great Britain by
Lowe & Brydone Printers Ltd
Thetford, Norfolk
© International Institute of Communications 1978

British Library Cataloguing in Publication Data

Fisher, Desmond
  Broadcasting in Ireland. - (Case studies on
  broadcasting systems).
  1. Broadcasting - Ireland
  I. Title II. Series
  384.54'09417   HE8689.9.17   77-30712

  ISBN 0 7100 8885 X

CONTENTS

FOREWORD

In many different parts of the world official and unofficial enquiries, often protracted, are being carried out concerning the future of broadcasting. Some of them have recently been completed. In every case two points have almost immediately become clear. First, the future of broadcasting can never be completely separated from its past, even thought the history of broadcasting in all countries is a recent one: there may be sharp breaks, not all of which are registered in legislation, but there are also continuities. Second, the future, like the past, will not depend on technological development alone. There are many exciting new communications technologies, many of them still in their early stages, but the speed and scope of their development will be determined by social, economic, political and cultural factors as well as by the technologies themselves. It has always been so.

Common technologies have been employed in different ways in different countries - sometimes with a few measures of control imposed by governments, by professional groups, or by trade unions, often with many. It is remarkable to what a great extent it is necessary to understand the general history of particular countries in order to understand what they have done with their conscious or unconscious communications policies.

This series of monographs, sponsored by the International Institute of Communications, is intended to direct attention to the main features of the communications patterns of a number of different countries. The studies deal with broadcasting structures rather than with the detailed processes of programme making or with the diffusion of news and ideas; and they seek first to explain how these structures came into existence, second, to identify what have been the landmarks in their histories, and, third, to elucidate what are the alternative possibilities envisaged for the future. Of course, a knowledge of the structures by itself is not enough to enable an adequate evaluation to be made of the quality of broadcasting output in any particular case. The same structure will generate different output at different times, and very similar structures will generate very different outputs.

Until recently it was thought possible to distinguish broadly between on the one hand systems controlled by government and on the other hand systems linked with business through private enterprise and advertising. Yet there was always a third type of system, represented formidably by the BBC, which entailed neither government control nor business underpinning. This system, which was widely copied, was seldom copied in its entirety, and it now has many variants, most of which have deviated substantially from the model. In many countries there are now dual or multiple systems, in some cases, but not in all, subject to common 'supervision'; and in all countries there are degrees and nuances of control of broadcasting output whether by governments or by market forces.

The United States system, which is important not only in itself but because of the influence it has through exports of programmes and through diffusion of broadcasting styles, is itself a complex system - containing as it does a multiplicity of agencies and a changing public service element. It is hoped that United States experience will be covered in a later volume. There is increasing pressure there for a major review in the light of that experience and of continuing technological change affecting not only broadcasting but a wide and increasingly interrelated group of new communications technologies.

Alongside complex national structures, the products of time and place and in many cases deeply resistant to fundamental change, there are, of course, many new broadcasting structures in the world, including many which have come into existence in recent years in new countries. Many of these structures reveal themselves as extremely complex, too, when they are subjected to careful scrutiny. Nor are they necessarily very malleable. The more governments set out to chart and carry through conscious 'communications policies' - often related directly to their planning policies - the more they are compelled to consider the relationship of 'traditional' modes of

communication to new technologies. The more, too, they
are forced to establish priorities. This series includes,
therefore, a number of countries where such policies have
been formulated or are in the course of formulation.

Measuring the distance between policy formulation and
policy implementation or effectiveness is, of course, at
least as difficult in this field as in any other, and
interesting work is being carried out by scholars in
several countries on promise and performance. This series
of studies, however, is less ambitious in intention. The
studies are designed to provide accessible and reliable
information rather than to evaluate the quality of
achievement. The first cases chosen include some where
there is no existing manageable monograph and some where
the particular experience of that country is of general
interest at the present time. The countries selected
include some which are old and some which are new, some
which are big and some which are small.

As the series unfolds, there will be increasing scope
for comparison and contrast, and international patterns
will doubtless be revealed - of 'models', of 'imports'
and 'exports', of regional 'exchanges', and of relationships between different media. As such comparison and
contrast become more sophisticated than they have been in
the past, any conclusions reached will be of increasing
value in the future to those policy makers who are concerned to see their own circumstances in perspective and
to frame their choices clearly.

Meanwhile, the International Institute of Communications, formerly called the International Broadcast Institute, which first launched this series, will continue to
concern itself with the general opportunities and problems
associated with the continuing advance of communications
technology. The Institute is an international body which
seeks to bring together engineers and social scientists,
lawyers and programme-makers, academics and administrators.

The author of each case study in this series has been
free to assemble and to present material relating to his
own country in a manner decided upon by him, and he alone
is responsible for the evidence offered and for the conclusions reached. Yet guidelines have been given him
about arrangement and coverage. Thus, he has been encouraged to ask questions as well as to compile facts. What
have been the critical points in the history of broadcasting? How have that history and the broadcasting

structures which have been evolved been related to the
history of other forms of communication (the Press, for
example)? What are the main institutional relationships
at the present time? What are likely to be the future
trends? Is it possible to talk of an integrated 'communications policy' in the case of the country under review?

The International Institute of Communications has no
views of its own as an institution on the answers to such
questions, but its Trustees and members believe that
answers should be forthcoming if debate is to be both
lively and well-informed. Much of the serious study of
communications systems has hitherto been carried out within the confines, cultural as well as political, of national boundaries, and it is such research which most easily
secures financial support. This series will point in a
different direction. It is not only comparison and contrast which are necessary but a grasp of what problems and
opportunities are common to countries, not necessarily
alone but in the great continental broadcasting unions or
other groupings between states.

We can now trace the beginnings of a 'global' sense
in communications studies. Indeed, the word 'beginning'
may be misleading. The sense certainly long preceded the
use of satellites and was anticipated in much of the
nineteenth-century literature. The world was being pulled
together; it was becoming a smaller place; everyone,
everywhere, it was suggested, would be drawn in, instant-
aneously.

Communications policies, of course, have often failed
to unite: instead, they have pulled people apart in
clashes of images as well as in wars of words. And some
of the case studies in this series will show how.

Two final points should be made. First, nothing stands
still in communications history, and there are bound to be
changes between the writing of these case studies and
their publication. The processes of implementation of
policy changes are often protracted. Second, it may well
be that we are moving out of the age of 'mass broadcasting' as we have understood it into a new age of electronic
communication. In that case, these studies will appear at
a strategic time and will deserve careful study separately
and together.

Asa Briggs
Worcester College, Oxford

ACKNOWLEDGMENTS

For assistance and advice in researching the appendices,
my thanks are due to Brian Mac Aongusa, Kathleen O'Brien,
Robert J. Collins and Mary Campbell of RTE.

The International Institute of Communications is most
grateful to the Hōsō-Bunka Foundation, Inc. for its
assistance in financing this series of case studies on
broadcasting systems.

INTRODUCTION

The world's first radio broadcast was made from Dublin,
Ireland, on Easter Tuesday, 25 April 1916. The occasion
was the Easter Week rising, an event which resulted six
years later in the winning of independence for those 26
of the island's 32 counties which are now the Republic of
Ireland.

The leaders of the rising, realising that the British
authorities would suppress or distort news of it dis-
patched by the normal channels, decided to send out the
information themselves. They occupied the Irish School
of Wireless Telegraphy, across the street from their headquarters in the General Post Office, and repaired a
damaged 1.5 kilowatt ship's transmitter which they found
there. From 5.30 p.m. that day until noon the next day,
when the building had to be abandoned, they sent out
signals in Morse code relaying communiqués issued by the
leaders of the rising.

The story of this episode is recounted by Maurice
Gorham, an Irishman who worked in the BBC for many years
before becoming Director of Broadcasting in Ireland. In
his history of the beginnings of sound broadcasting in
Ireland (1967), he writes (p. 2):
> This was not broadcasting as we know it, for wireless
> telephony was not yet available and Morse messages were
> all that could be sent out. But it was news by wire-
> less, not aimed at any known receiver but sent out
> broadcast, and that was a new idea in 1916.

The account is verified by no less an authority than
Marshall McLuhan (1964). He writes (p. 304):
> That [1916] was the year of the Irish Easter rebellion
> and of the first radio broadcast. Wireless had already

been used on ships as ship-to-shore 'telegraph'. The
Irish rebels used a ship's wireless to make, not a
point-to-point message, but a diffused broadcast in the
hope of getting word to some ship that would relay
their story to the American press.

It was, however, to be another ten years before the
Irish radio service was opened. This was on 1 January
1926, four years after ratification of the Anglo-Irish
treaty had ended the war of independence. Since then, the
development of radio, and later of television, has been
bound up with building the political, economic and social
framework of the new state and it is against this background that the evolution of the broadcasting system in
Ireland has to be viewed.

What makes the present Irish broadcasting situation
relevant to outsiders, is that it is contending with some
of the most difficult problems facing broadcasters everywhere and which, perhaps, exist in Ireland in greater
numbers and in a more complicated form than elsewhere.
Such, at least, is the view from inside the Irish context.

Other countries, such as Britain and Denmark, have
economic problems which impinge on broadcasting. Ireland
is the least well-off country in the EEC. Its per capita
gnp is less than two-fifths that of Denmark and less than
two-thirds that of the UK. Broadcasting in Ireland has
inevitably felt the consequences.

The Belgians have a language problem? So have the
Irish, perhaps not as bad since no one has been killed
over it, but one which has created a national dilemma and
a major area of concern for the broadcasting service.

The Dutch, the Swiss and the Canadian broadcasting
organisations have to compete against the services of
more powerful neighbours? The Irish national broadcasting
service, Radio Telefís Eireann (RTE), competes in half its
television reception area (44 per cent of householders)
against, arguably, the two best broadcasting systems in
the world, BBC and IBA.

The Austrians, the French and many others have had to
cope with political repercussions in broadcasting? The
Irish service has experienced a judicial inquiry into one
of its programmes, many parliamentary attacks and the dismissal of its entire governing board in 1972.

Finally, broadcasting everywhere is being criticised by sociologists and by audiences? There is probably no more critical audience than the Irish of whom Samuel Johnson, of dictionary fame, once accurately, if spitefully, said: 'The Irish are a fair people; they never speak well of one another.'

Besides these problems, which affect broadcasting more directly, Ireland has been going through structural and sociological changes which have had a less direct but important influence on the development of the broadcasting system.

In many ways, Ireland is still adjusting to the consequences of regaining her independence after centuries of outside control. Many of the assumptions and ambitions which were formerly taken for granted have been modified or discarded. The earlier visions, held by some of the founding-fathers, of a united, Gaelic-speaking, simple-living, pastoral community have vanished. The re-unification of the island, partitioned temporarily (as it was thought) in 1920, seems further from attainment now than it did then. Any possibility of saving the Irish language could soon disappear. The demand for material well being is as strong in Ireland as anywhere else in Europe. Supermarkets, housing estates and factories are spreading into the green fields.

As is so often the case, political independence is only a step on the road to creating a unified, prosperous nation with a strong sense of self-identity and self-respect. Ireland had also to embark on a process of freeing herself from economic, psychological and cultural over-dependence on Britain and of developing a viable economy, a full sense of identity and a fully Irish culture, open to outside influences but strong enough, where necessary, to deflect or repeal alien cultural forms.

That process is still continuing and it is as part of it that the Irish broadcasting experience is most appropriately understood.

Chapter 1

THE IRISH ENVIRONMENT FOR BROADCASTING

1 GEOGRAPHY AND HISTORY

Ireland is a small island, lying to the extreme north-west
of the European continent. It is only 300 miles (480 kms)
long and 150 miles (240 kms) wide, with a total area of
32,595 sq. miles (84,421 sq. kms) the same size as Austria
or the State of Maine, New England.

Physically, the country is saucer-shaped. The large
limestone central plain, mostly grassland and peat bog, is
fringed with coastal highlands of old red sandstone, gran-
ite and basalt. The highest mountain - Carrantuohill, Co.
Kerry - is 3,414 feet (1,040 metres): the longest river -
the Shannon - is 230 miles (370 kms) long, and the biggest
lake - Lough Neagh - is 153 sq. miles (396 sq. kms) in
area.

The climate, influenced by the Gulf Stream and the pre-
vailing mild south-westerly winds, is temperate (4°C to
16°C on average) and, with no place more than 70 miles
from the sea, temperatures are fairly uniform over the
country. The rainfall is comparatively high (40-60 inches
a year): this produces the green grass for which Ireland
is famous.

Small as it is, the island is politically divided.
The Republic of Ireland, which is the subject of this
study, is a sovereign, independent state, consisting of
26 of the 32 counties in the island. The other 6 counties
of Northern Ireland constitute an integral part of the
United Kingdom of Great Britain and Northern Ireland.

Small as it is, too, Ireland has a complicated history;
partly glorious, mostly tragic. The consciousness of that

history is always close to the surface, affecting the present and shaping the future. To understand the Irish situation today, even in such areas as broadcasting policy and development, it is necessary to look back, if only superficially, at the past.

Early society

Ireland was first populated about 6000 BC. Some of the finest archaeological remains - megalithic passage-graves, dolmens and standing stones - date from c. 3000 BC.

The last of successive waves of Celtic invaders arrived about 100 BC. They spoke what scholars call a Q-Celtic language, as distinct from the P-Celtic tongue of earlier invaders. From it developed the Irish language spoken as the vernacular until the mid-nineteenth century. Efforts to restore it to common use have political overtones today and, as will be seen, a bearing on broadcasting policy.

Early Irish society was based on the 'tuath', an extended family unit, under a chief, called a 'rí'. It had a highly developed system of laws administered by experts, music, poetry, competitive games, including funeral games on the Homeric pattern, and literary contests. An ancient system of writing, called Ogham, consisting of lines carved on the angles of pillar stones, was used for special - mainly commemorative - purposes.

The 'Golden Age'

Though Ireland had regular contact with Roman Britain, the legions never crossed the narrow seas. And as they were withdrawn to meet the barbarian attacks, Irish warrior-bands raided deep into the empire. On one such raid, probably in Britain, a youth, who was later to be Ireland's patron saint, was captured.

St Patrick and other missionary bishops - Palladius arrived in Ireland in 431 AD, Patrick in 432 AD - had great success in converting the Irish to the Christian faith. Monasteries and schools of learning, which attracted thousands of students from all parts of Europe, sprang up throughout Ireland. And, as the Roman empire in the west crumbled, Irish monks and scholars flocked into Europe - to Scotland, England, France, Germany, Austria, Italy, even as far as Kiev - to keep Christianity and learning alive.

It was Ireland's golden age and the scholars called her
'the island of saints and scholars'.

English rule

From the ninth century to the eleventh, Viking raiders
from Scandinavia terrorised Ireland, repeatedly sacking
and looting the monasteries and schools. They established
the first towns, remaining there as the leading traders
after their military power was broken in 1014. But before
a centralised Irish nation could be created from the contending 'kingdoms', the Normans landed in 1169 and a long
and tragic period in Irish history began. In the following centuries, until almost the present day, the history
of Ireland and the whole life of the Irish people were to
be dominated by her nearest neighbour, Britain.

First the Norman barons, and soon the English kings,
expropriated the lands of the Irish. Warfare was almost
continuous until the last of the great Irish chieftains
fled in 1607 and the old Gaelic order, which had survived
practically intact for longer than history records, was
finally shattered. Successive 'plantations' banished
thousands from their ancestral lands, Oliver Cromwell
giving them the stark choice of 'To hell or Connacht',
that is, death or banishment to the bogs and mountains of
the western province. Rebellion followed rebellion until
in 1800 the separate Irish parliament was abolished and
Ireland became an integral part of the United Kingdom of
Great Britain and Ireland.

Further efforts, both constitutional and revolutionary,
finally succeeded in gaining independence for the 26
counties which, under the name of the Irish Free State,
became in 1922 a dominion of the British Commonwealth.
Ratification of the Anglo-Irish treaty, which ended the
war of independence, was followed by a civil war, lasting
from July 1922 to August 1923 and ending in victory for
the pro-treaty side. The division created then has con-
stituted the main political dividing line until the present day.

The 1937 Constitution made Ireland a republic in all
but name; in 1948, the External Relations Act, under which
Ireland recognised the British sovereign as head of the
Commonwealth, was repealed; and on 18 April 1949, the
Republic of Ireland was officially declared.

Special relationship

Britain's long political, commercial and cultural dominance in Ireland was underpinned by control of the communications systems. For political reasons, the Irish language was deliberately and systematically destroyed as the
spoken tongue. British newsagency and newspaper channels
mediated to Ireland knowledge of events in the world and,
with a few notable exceptions, carried, suppressed or doc-
tored to suit British interests reports of happenings in
Ireland. Arthur Griffith, one of the founders of the
modern Irish state, could complain justifiably about the
'paper wall' screening news into and out of Ireland.

The effects of the British connection still influence
many aspects of Irish life. English has almost totally
supplanted Irish as the common language. Britain is by
far Ireland's largest supplier and biggest market. Irish
boys hero-worship English soccer stars as well as the
leading players of the Irish games of hurling and Gaelic
football. In many areas of law, social reform, technology,
organisation and communication, what Britain does today
Ireland does years later.

A major influence is the penetration of British television into a large part of Ireland. Signals from BBC
and ITV can be received, with high-gain rooftop aerials
or via cable systems, in an area of about one-third the
country containing half the population.

History has thus created between the two countries a
relationship which is probably unique. No passport is
required for travel between the two countries. Irish
citizens in Britain have automatic residence, including
voting rights. The Irish and British £s have so far
maintained parity.

The way the British and Irish view one another almost
defies rational analysis. It has been said, with some
truth, that 'the trouble with the English is that they
can't remember; the trouble with the Irish is that they
can't forget'. Yet without some appreciation of the factors which have created the relationship between them, it
is impossible to understand much of what is happening in
Ireland today, including developments in broadcasting.

2   CONSTITUTION AND ADMINISTRATION

Ireland is a parliamentary democracy, the present constitution having been adopted in a referendum in 1937. An
elected Uachtarán (President) is head of state and the
Taoiseach (Prime Minister) is head of government. The
President has limited powers but is seen as the guardian
of the constitution. There is a bicameral parliament, the
Dáil (lower house) with 148 seats and the Seanad (upper
house) with 60. Members of the Dáil are elected by universal adult (18) suffrage under a proportional represent-
ation voting system with a single transferable vote.
Forty-three of the 60 members of the Seanad are elected
to represent various vocational and cultural interests,
6 represent the universities and 11 are appointed by the
Taoiseach.

The Dáil is elected for a maximum period of five years
but may be dissolved earlier by presidential proclamation
at the request of the Taoiseach; the President has discretion to refuse the Taoiseach's request following a
government defeat on a confidence motion. A general election for the Seanad must take place within ninety days of
the dissolution of the Dáil.

The government, which is collectively responsible to
Dáil Eireann for conducting the affairs of state, consists of 7-15 cabinet ministers (in 1977, 15), each of
whom normally heads at least one department. They are
appointed by the Taoiseach and must resign when he does.
The Minister for Posts and Telegraphs has parliamentary
accountability for broadcasting.

There are three main political parties. The largest
is Fianna Fáil (literally Warriors of Destiny), founded by
Mr Eamon de Valera in 1926 from the side which lost the
civil war. It was in office during the periods 1932-48,
1951-4, 1957-73 and since 1977 to date. The second largest party is Fine Gael (People of Ireland), which governed
from 1922-32 under the name of Cumann na nGaedheal (Association of the Irish) and in coalition with the Labour
Party, the third largest party, from 1948-51, 1954-7 and
1973-7.

Local government

At the local government level, Ireland has a system of
county councils, county borough corporations, borough

corporations, urban district councils and boards of town commissioners. These are elected bodies responsible for services like planning and development of roads and bridges, housing, sanitary and fire services, public amenities and public assistance. The executive functions are exercised by county managers, who are responsible for day-to-day administration of the local authorities' affairs.

3   POPULATION TRENDS

The population of the whole island of Ireland is about 4.7 million, of whom 3.12 million are in the Republic. This represents a density of 44 per sq. km., by far the lowest in the EEC and only one-seventh that of Belgium and the Netherlands.

   In 1841, the total population was some 8.5 million. The terrible famine of 1845-8, caused by successive failures of the potato crop, left 800,000 dead of starvation. In a decade, 2.5 million emigrated, 1 million of them to the USA, with one in six dying of plague on the 'coffinships'. The famine had a traumatic effect on Ireland and emigration subsequently became a major feature of Irish life. Between 1848 and 1914, over 4 million emigrated: in the decade after the Second World War the annual average was 40,000.

   In recent years, the trend has been reversed. The economic boom of the 1960s attracted home to Ireland thousands who had emigrated and kept at home young men and women who in other times would have left. The recession of the mid-1970s had a similar effect. With high unemployment in the UK, the main outlet for emigrants in the twentieth century, thousands more unemployed emigrants returned home to live on family farms and first-time emigration practically ceased. All the time, the rate of natural increase (the ratio of births over deaths) continued high by general developed nation standards.

   The result has been that the net population increase, which had been -4.9 per 1,000 inhabitants in 1951-61, jumped to +11 per 1,000 in the following decade, 1961-71. The 1976 census was cancelled for economy reasons, but the trend is likely to have at least doubled in the period since 1971. One authoritative projection indicates a population increase of between 18 and 27 per cent in the 1971-86 period, with half the population under 25 years of age by the end of the period.

The overall picture is one of a steadily increasing
total population, with a possible doubling of the numbers
of young married couples over the years to 1986, with a
significant internal shift from the rural areas to the
major towns and cities and with a continuing 9 per cent of
under-sixteens and over-65s (42 per cent in 1973).

Town v. country

The urbanisation which followed the industrial revolution
in Britain did not affect Ireland.   Town-dwelling had
never been a feature of the traditional Irish way of life,
the cities and towns having been founded by the Norse and
Norman invaders and inhabited by their descendants.   At
the time of the 1845-8 famine, 85 per cent of the population still lived on the land: by 1914, the figure was still
as high as 65 per cent.

The move to the towns roughly coincided with the coming
of independence.   Dublin, which as seat of the Irish parliament in the eighteenth century had been, after London,
the biggest centre in Britain and Ireland and one of
Europe's finest cities, began to recover from its nine-
teenth century decline.   Once again a seat of government,
it developed commercially and culturally.   Today, about
half the Republic's total population lives in the eastern
province of Leinster and half of those, that is 25 per
cent of the total, lives in greater Dublin area (population: 850,000).   The other larger cities are Cork
(134,000), Limerick (64,000), Waterford (35,000), Galway
(30,000).   But Irish towns are small and nearly half of
the population still lives in communities of under 1,500
persons.

Dublin's size creates an economic, cultural and administrative imbalance as well as a demographic one.   It has
resulted in a city versus countryside polarisation which
is beginning to be reflected in an anti-farmer attitude
in the cities, especially Dublin, and an anti-urban worker
bias among the farming community.   It is reflected also in
a degree of rural antagonism to what is regarded as a
Dublin-dominated broadcasting system and Dublin-oriented
programming.

This urban-rural divide is the most marked sociological
watershed in Ireland.   There are no ethnic minorities:
the assimilation of the earliest settlers, whose origin
is unknown, with various Celtic tribes and later with the

Norse and the Anglo-Normans is long ago complete in what
is now the Republic. The Norse left few traces except in
placenames and the Norman-English were so successfully
absorbed that they became 'more Irish than the Irish themselves' and from comparatively early on shared the Irish
nationalist tradition.

Denominational percentages

In the Republic, too, religious differences have almost
ceased to count, the Protestant denominations suffering
no political, economic or cultural discrimination and no
longer identifying themselves with Britain. In an effort
to remove any appearance of state favouritism, a constitutional provision (article 44.1.2) recognising 'the special
position of the Holy Catholic Apostolic and Roman Church
as the guardian of the Faith professed by the great
majority' was removed by a referendum in 1972.

    Roman Catholics form 94 per cent of the population in
the Republic and about one-third of the population in
Northern Ireland. The largest Protestant denomination in
the Republic is the Church of Ireland (3.2 per cent)
followed by Presbyterian (0.5 per cent), Methodists (0.2
per cent) and others (0.3 per cent). The remainder (1.8
per cent) are either of no religion or supply no information.

    In Northern Ireland, the Presbyterians, with 27 per
cent of the total population, form the largest Protestant
denomination, followed by Church of Ireland (22 per cent)
and Methodist (5 per cent).

4   ECONOMY

By world standards, Ireland is reckoned among the developed nations. Certainly, the Irish eat well: their average
daily calorie intake is among the world's highest. By
'western' standards, however, Ireland is a poor country,
coming fourth-last in the OECD's 24-country gnp per capita
table for 1975.

    The main structural defect in the Irish economy has
traditionally been the lack of industry and stagnation in
agriculture. Under British rule, industry was stifled to
prevent it harming British interests: agriculture was
crippled by oppressive 'rack' rents and insecurity of

tenure. Between 1848 and 1914, the gnp increased by only
0.5 per cent per annum, the lowest in western Europe.

Since independence, the challenge has been to provide
industrial jobs for people leaving the land at an annual
average rate of 2.75 per cent. It has been done - just -
for those who did not emigrate, by a combination of high
tariffs and, later, by attractive incentives to foreign
manufacturers.

State bodies

Though private enterprise was encouraged, only state
initiative could meet the biggest economic challenges
facing the country in its early years of development.
State-sponsored organisations were established to run
insurance, electricity, sugar and steel production, transport, the promotion of tourism, of exports, of industrial
development and of sea and inland fisheries, industrial
financing and many other aspects of the economy. Some
of them were set up as statutory corporations, others as
public or private companies with varying degrees of state
financing and control.

There are now some one hundred such bodies, employing
about 65,000 people, with total net assets of over
£1,000 million and an annual turnover of well over £500
million. In 1960, Radio Telefís Éireann, the national
broadcasting service, was established as one such statutory corporation 'to establish and maintain a national
television and sound broadcasting service'.

Because external trade represents 90 per cent of her
gnp, Ireland was badly hit by the post-1973 recession. In
1976, unemployment at over 10 per cent and inflation at 18
per cent were among the highest in the EEC and among the
worst in the OECD. Though unemployment is likely to stay
high for some years, the upward swing of the economy,
which began in 1958, is beginning to resume.

In 55 years, however, a great deal has been achieved.
EEC membership from 1973 has greatly increased farm in-
comes and industry is growing stronger. Housing and
social welfare standards are improving steadily. Annual
consumption per capita in 1975 averaged US $ 1,542: there
were 157 passenger cars, 120 telephones, 176 television
sets and 1.2 doctors per 1,000 inhabitants. Average
annual increase in wages between 1970 and 1975 was 19.7

per cent. Despite continuing structural weaknesses, Ireland now knows a prosperity she has not known for many
centuries. The traditional one-storey Irish cottage, of
whitewashed mud walls and thatched roof, is a museum piece
and an Irish village can no longer be fairly described as
consisting of 'a dozen inhabited houses, a dozen ruined
houses and half-a-dozen pubs'.

5 EDUCATION

Under the constitution (article 42.1) the Irish state
'acknowledges that the primary and natural educator of
the child is the family and guarantees to respect the
inalienable right and duty of parents to provide, according to their means, for the religious and moral, intellec-
tual, physical and social education of their children.'

   Education at primary and post-primary level is free and
financial assistance is available, subject to a means
test, to third-level students who reach a certain educational standard. Education between the ages of six and
fifteen is compulsory, though the great majority of children start school in their fifth year.

   For historical reasons, the Irish educational system is
complex in its organisation and largely denominational in
character. With the consolidation of English power in
Ireland in the seventeenth century, the old monastic and
bardic schools were finally suppressed and for most of the
eighteenth century Catholic education was proscribed.
Students, if they were poor, attended clandestine 'hedge
schools' at the side of the road; if rich, they went
abroad to one of about twenty special colleges for Irish
students established in Belgium, France, Spain, Portugal,
Italy and in Prague.

   Parish schools founded by Henry VIII to make English
the spoken tongue had not succeeded and after 1831, by
which time the anti-Catholic laws had been repealed or
relaxed, they were replaced by a system of national
schools. These were not state schools as such: the
government, through a board of governors, distributed
grants to supplement local contributions to voluntary
parochial schools, founded by the Catholic and Protestant
authorities. The principle thus established of denominational schools with state support but not state management
still applies over much of the educational system in
Ireland.

Present-day primary schools are provided through a combination of local contributions - usually a site and a
proportion of the capital cost - and state support, which
includes a large part of the capital cost as well as the
cost of maintenance and of teachers' salaries. Ownership
is vested in local trustees who operate through boards of
management, representing the trustees, the parents and the
teachers. In the case of Catholic schools, the parish
priest is usually the chairman of the management board.
The board appoints the teachers and runs the school subject to close departmental control of the curriculum and
standards of teaching. Almost all the primary schools are
denominational and about 95 per cent of all primary-level
schoolchildren attend them.

Most children go on to at least some years of second-
level schooling and about half of all children over 15
complete post-primary education. The post-primary system
caters for children of approximately twelve to nineteen
years of age and includes secondary schools, vocational
schools, comprehensive schools and community schools.
Regional technical colleges cater for the senior cycle of
second-level and for some third-level students. About
70 per cent of the full-time students of the post-primary
age group attend secondary schools; 20 per cent vocational
schools and the remaining 10 per cent are divided among
the other types of schools.

The secondary schools, which developed from institutions founded by local laymen and clergy in the nine-
teenth century, are denominationally owned, the great
majority by Catholic religious orders. They now also
receive most of their financing from the State, which
also prescribes the curriculum. They are generally organised in two cycles - the junior cycle (12-15 years) leading to the Intermediate Certificate examination and the
senior cycle (16-18 years) leading to the Leaving Certificate.

Vocational schools are financed partly by local authorities and partly from central funds and provide education
with a technical or practical basis. The schools are man-
aged by committees elected by the local authority for the
area.

Comprehensive schools are a comparatively new introduction, dating from 1966. They aim at combining academic
and vocational instruction at secondary level in one curriculum. Management is by committees representing the

religious authorities, the local vocational education committee and the Minister for Education.

Community schools are a still later development. They follow the same general lines as comprehensive schools but are usually formed from the amalgamation of existing secondary and vocational schools in a particular area and also cater for adult and general part-time education. Management is by boards representing the secondary school managers, the local vocational education committee and the parents.

Regional technical colleges offer whole-time or part-time instruction with an emphasis on technical and commercial subjects, ranging from craft to professional level.

Some 12 per cent of post-primary level students of all categories go on for third-level education. This level includes universities, teacher training schools and technological and technical institutions. A better basis for international comparison is provided by the calculation that about 35 per cent of secondary school students, that is, those with an academic background, go on to the universities, a figure which is well up to European average. The figure would be much higher but for a shortage of university places and university entrance has deliberately to be kept down by stiff qualification requirements.

There are two universities in Dublin and others in Cork, Galway and Maynooth. The senior foundation in Dublin is Trinity College, established under Elizabeth 1 in 1591 to promote English culture and Protestantism. Until 1793, Catholics were forbidden entry; from then until 1970, they were discouraged by their own bishops from attending. Catholics now number 60 per cent of the student body.

The second Dublin foundation, University College, was established in 1851 as the Catholic University of Ireland. It and the university colleges in Cork and Galway, both founded in 1845, were incorporated as 'constituent colleges' into the National University of Ireland in 1908. Later, six 'recognised colleges' were brought into the university system, including St Patrick's College, Maynooth, founded in 1795 for the education of Catholics and since 1817 the main Catholic seminary in Ireland. Both universities are self-governing but receive annual grants from central funds. Government proposals for the reorganisation of the system into five independent universities at Dublin (2), Cork, Galway and Maynooth have yet to be implemented.

The share of the gnp represented by expenditure on public education (80 per cent of total educational expenditure) more than doubled in the decade to 1977. The number of full-time pupils in second-level doubled and in third-level increased by 70 per cent.

In 1976, the numbers in full-time education were
first-level   - 550,078
second-level   - 271,098
third-level   - 33,636

Media education

In recent years, with an increasing public awareness of the importance of the media in creating or, at least, reinforcing attitudes, education in understanding them has begun to find a place in the overall education system. Since 1974, media education has been part of the curriculum in a transition year project currently being piloted in some seventeen schools in Ireland. The transition year, an extra year of education following completion of the junior cycle in second-level schools and involving schoolchildren in the 15-16 year age group, is designed to provide an opportunity for self-development, in an atmosphere removed from examination pressures, for those intending to leave full-time education at 16 or for those continuing into the senior cycle of the post-primary system. As part of a wide curriculum designed as 'education for life', students learn about the print media, especially newspapers, and about radio and television. They are helped to evaluate editorials and programmes both by developing thinking skills and by themselves producing magazines and making radio and television programmes on amateur or semi-professional equipment. While the project is still in an early stage, the response to it is enough to convince educators that it is worthwhile. Individual schools have also developed media education to a considerable degree of sophistication.

It is Department of Education policy to encourage the inclusion of media education in the compulsory civics course in second-level schools: at more senior levels, media education is part of the curriculum for trainee-journalists and participants in adult education courses. The professional diploma course in journalism at the College of Commerce, Rathmines, Dublin, includes lectures dealing with the process and techniques of communication, its cultural implications, the influence of the media and the assumptions of the media-consumer, violence (especially in the Irish context) as portrayed in the media, balance in communication and bias in the communicator, advertising, access broadcasting and audience analysis. Since this course provides the main catchment area for recruits to journalism in Ireland, the media education aspect is important.

Media courses at the People's College, under the auspices of the Irish Congress of Trade Unions, are designed to give participants, mainly trade unionists, an understanding of how the media, particularly press, radio and television, affect their lives. Lectures deal with, inter alia, advertising, news, interviewing techniques, the media and children, radio in a television age and the cultural and other effects of future media developments.

Media education plays an important part in a new diploma course for adult education, the first full-time professional course of its kind in Ireland, initiated in 1976-7 at St Patrick's College, Maynooth. Aimed at adult educators, community development officers and out-of-school youth educators, the course deals with the nature, extent, use and influence of the mass media in adult education; analyses media influence in human, social and community behaviour; gives practical instruction in media techniques and studies media use in solving social problems such as illiteracy and Third World poverty.

Special media courses are conducted at the Communications Centre, under the auspices of the Catholic hierarchy at Booterstown, Co. Dublin. The course covers popular literature, pop music, newspapers, film drama, radio and television. Special one-day courses for senior students cover some of the same ground and involve participants in making a news bulletin with professional studio equipment.

Educational broadcasting

Both schools broadcasts and adult education and enrichment programming are provided on RTE. Schools broadcasting is part-financed by the Department of Education but in recent years the State's economic difficulties caused the department to reduce and eventually, in 1976-7, to withdraw its financing. RTE is continuing a limited schools service, particularly on television. Adult education and enrichment programmes are carried regularly on both radio and television.

6   CULTURE

In some areas, Ireland has made a much greater contribution to world culture than her small population, disturbed history and economic difficulties might have suggested was likely.

Some scholars claim that Ireland is the first nation north of the Alps to have produced a vernacular literature. From the eighth century and, probably, earlier, the monastic schools were writing down in the Irish language the legends, sagas, hero tales, family genealogies, poetry and historical accounts handed down for centuries by the high-caste bards and professional poets of the old Gaelic order. This magnificent corpus of literature is, inevitably, not well known internationally except in academic and literary circles. But a long literary tradition in English stretches from Swift via Goldsmith, Sheridan, George Moore, Shaw, Wilde, W.B. Yeats, Joyce to Frank O'Connor and Brendan Behan in more recent times.

In painting, Walter Osborne, Jack B. Yeats, Sir William Orpen, Sir John Lavery, Sarah Purser, Gerard Dillon, George Campbell, Louis le Brocquy, Sean Keating and Arthur Armstrong are internationally known; in stained glass Evie Hone and Harry Clarke; while John Field (composer of the first nocturne), Balfe (The Bohemian Girl) and Wallace (Maritana) are still remembered in international music circles. The world-famous Abbey Theatre was founded in 1904, producing dramatists like Synge, Lady Gregory, Sean O'Casey, Brian Friel and Denis Johnston, and a string of well-known actors. More recently, there has been a remarkable revival of traditional Irish music, singing and dancing and amateur dramatics.

The cultural renaissance which began at the turn of the century combined the romanticism and the realism of the nationalist revival which was to culminate in the 1916 Easter Rising and the eventual winning of independence for what is now the Republic. The radio service, which began in 1926, drew heavily on this tradition.

Press

Newspaper circulation in Ireland is relatively high.
Daily (i.e. morning and evening) circulation, including
British dailies, is 243 copies per 1,000 people; non-daily
(including Sunday) newspaper circulation is about 486 per
1,000.   Sixty per cent of the adult population read an
Irish morning paper, 82 per cent an Irish Sunday paper and
62 per cent a provincial weekly newspaper.   In addition,
there is a wide variety of magazines, mainly serving
special-interest readership.

The first Irish newsheet appeared in 1659 and the first
commercial newspaper in 1662.   The eighteenth and nine-
teenth centuries saw periodic bursts of publishing both in
Dublin and in the provinces.   The first provincial paper
was founded in 1766 (it is still publishing thrice
weekly) and in 1870 there were 103 local and provincial
publications, many of them barely able to survive.   Today,
there are some 42 provincial weeklies with a total circulation of 550,000, four times that of 100 years ago.

Dublin has three morning newspapers (total circulation
330,000), two evenings (275,000) and three Sundays (about
1,000,000); Cork has a morning (65,000) and evening
(37,000) paper.   British newspapers sell about 53,000
copies daily and over 500,000 on Sundays, i.e. 11 per cent
of the morning newspaper market and 35 per cent of the
Sunday market.

One of the Dublin groups - Irish Press Ltd - was
started in 1931 by Mr Éamon de Valera, founder of the
Fianna Fáil party; a second group, Independent Newspapers,
which has taken over several provincial papers, was
founded in 1905.   The third, the 'Irish Times', was founded in 1859.   The Cork morning newspaper dates back to
1841.

Books

The relatively small market in Ireland limits the scale
of book publishing.   In 1975, the last year for which
statistics are available, 752 new titles were published,
an increase of 25 on the previous year.   Of the 307
publishers represented, 188 were based in Dublin, 77 in
other centres of the Republic and 42 in Northern Ireland.
Twenty-five Irish-language publishers issued 83 titles.
The overall total includes pamphlets brought out by minor

publishers, including some private individuals.

The Irish Book Publishers' Association has 32 corporate
members, of which some 15 are full-scale publishing companies, though small by international standards. Probably
no more than four or five publishing houses in Ireland
have an annual turnover in excess of £500,000 and among
them they account for the bulk of book publishing both
educational and general.

The Dewey classification breakdown of titles published
in 1975 is:

000	Biography and general works	13
100	Philosophy and psychology	6
200	Religion and theology	42
300	Social science and government	196
S.T.	School textbooks	102
400	Language and philosophy	16
500	Pure sciences	20
600	Technology, medicine and business	38
700	Music, art and recreation	80
800	Literature and criticism	116
900	History, biography and geography	77

Cinema

Cinema attendances in Ireland peaked about 1957 but both
the number of cinemas and the number of attendances have
about halved in the twenty years since. There are recent
signs of improvement in attendances, especially among the
younger (15-34) age groups for whom, in the absence of
other social amenities, cinema-going is an important
activity.

Films

Newsreels were being made in Ireland at the beginning of
the century and there are at present several documentary
and short-film producers, some of whose work has won
international notice. So far, the lack of a large enough
market has delayed the development of a full-scale film
industry. But legislation to establish a film industry
board is being prepared and the government has acquired,
through a state-sponsored company, a major film studio
complex near Dublin which it is running as a production
centre in the meantime. Taxation advantages are available
to foreign film makers.

7   TELECOMMUNICATIONS

Four years after Bell's invention, the first telephone
exchange, with five subscribers, was opened in Dublin in
1880.   By 1 April 1922, when the transfer from the British
Postmaster-General to the new Irish administration took
place, 194 exchanges, 533 call offices and 12,500 subscribers were included in the handover.   Successive
development programmes have brought the total to about
400,000 subscribers, almost half of them in the greater
Dublin area, with 1,034 telephone exchanges and 1,285
telegraph offices.   Subscriber trunk dialling is available
to 87 per cent of subscribers and international subscriber
dialling to about 50 per cent, being available from Dublin
and Shannon to 21 overseas countries, including most of
western Europe and North America.   The Irish authorities
have 32 satellite circuits, via Goonhilly earth station in
Cornwall, England, to the USA and Australia.   In 1976, a
total of over 500 million telephone calls was made.

The international telex exchange in Dublin, opened in
1974, was the first fully electronic, stored-programme-
controlled telex exchange in Europe.   The national telex
system is completely automatic with automatic service also
to nearly all countries with modern systems.   Data transmission is also provided and Ireland is part of Euronet,
the EEC's computerised information network, and of the
Eurodata Foundation for market studies in the field of
data communication.

Ireland is a member of the International Telecommunications Union (ITU) and of the Conference of European Postal
and Telecommunications Administrations (CEPT).   All telecommunications in Ireland are operated by the Department
of Posts and Telegraphs, of which the Minister for Posts
and Telegraphs is the political head.   The Minister has
parliamentary accountability for radio and television,
though broadcasting operations are the responsibility of
the statutory body, Radio Telefís Éireann, subject to
certain powers which are specifically reserved to the
Minister or the government.

The microwave link system for broadcasting was built
between 1961 and 1963 and renewed in 1975-8.   With the
exception of the output link, owned and maintained by
RTE, the network is provided and maintained by the
Department of Posts and Telegraphs and leased to RTE at an
annual rent.   RTE and the BBC jointly own a microwave link
between Mohercrom, Co. Cavan, in the Republic and Belfast

in Northern Ireland: this is RTE's connection to the
Eurovision network.

Chapter 2

EVOLUTION OF BROADCASTING IN IRELAND

1 RADIO

Despite her claims to a broadcasting 'first' in 1916,
Ireland was not involved in the beginnings of radio broadcasting proper in the early 1920s. For the first two
years of the decade, she was fighting a war of independence; in 1922-3, she was involved in a bitter civil war.
In the circumstances, applications from Irish and British
companies (including the Marconi company and the 'Daily
Express') for a broadcasting licence were refused.

At the end of 1923, six months after the civil war
ended, a white paper proposed for Ireland a system like
that which resulted in the formation of the British Broadcasting Company, the forerunner of the BBC. This was a
consortium of interested manufacturers and importers of
radio sets and components.

Dáil Éireann, however, recognising the potentialities
of radio both in fostering and integrating Irish culture
and protecting it from what were regarded at the time as
harmful outside influences, especially from Britain,
recommended that 'broadcasting should be a State service
purely - the installation and the working of it to be
solely in the hands of the Postal Ministry'. As a result,
the Wireless Telegraphy Act of 1926 provided for 'the
establishment and maintenance of State broadcasting stations', the service to be financed from licence fees,
advertising and import duties on wireless sets and components. The act defined 'wireless telegraphy', in a manner
which might now, in the light of the discovery of television, be thought far-sighted, as 'any system of communi-
cating messages, spoken words, music, images, pictures,
prints or other communications, sounds, signs or signals

by means of radiated electro-magnetic waves.'

Modest beginnings

Because of the young nation's scarce finances, the beginnings of the Irish radio service were modest. A 1 kw
transmitter was installed in a wooden hut alongside police
barracks in Dublin with an aerial system mounted on wooden
masts. Offices and a studio were acquired over an employment exchange in the city centre. In November 1925, a
director was appointed and on 1 January 1926 2RN opened
with a speech by Dr Douglas Hyde, later first President
of Ireland, which was relayed by the BBC's new 25 kw
transmitter 5XX at Daventry.

A capacity to improvise and to cope with emergencies is
a common Irish quality and it was heavily depended on in
the early days. The Irish station claimed to have been
the first broadcasting service outside the USA to have
relayed a live commentary on a sporting event (on 29
August 1926). And 2RN was the first to announce Lind-
bergh's successful New York to Paris crossing of the
Atlantic on 20-1 May 1927.

The greatest difficulty in the early days was fighting
the parsimonious civil service bureaucracy, inevitable in
the circumstances of the time, which made staffing and
financing operations difficult. The operating budget was
£120 for a seven-day week, including fees for relays and
copyright.

National service

In 1927, a subsidiary 1 kw station was opened in Cork (the
studios closed down again from 1930-58) and in 1928 the
Dublin studios moved into new premises in the reconstruc-
ted General Post Office, wrecked by British artillery
during the 1916 Easter week rising.

A high-power - 60 kw, later increased to 100 kw -
station, used briefly during the World Eucharistic Congress in Dublin in June 1932, was formally opened in
February 1933, at Athlone, Co. Westmeath. This meant that
broadcasting in Ireland, hitherto largely confined to the
Dublin and Cork areas, became a national service. The
Athlone transmitter was renewed in 1955 and remained the
main RTE transmitter until 1975, when it was replaced by a

new 500 kw transmitter at Tullamore, Co. Offaly.

In 1939, efforts to launch a short-wave service had to
be postponed because of the Second World War and were
abandoned in 1948. In anticipation of this new service,
aimed mainly at Irish people in the USA, the broadcasting
infrastructure had been enormously strengthened. The
staff was doubled and new equipment provided. Maurice
Gorham wrote (1967, p. 162):

> Radio Éireann gained - and never lost - a proper news
> service, a Symphony Orchestra, a Light Orchestra,
> staff script-writers, outside broadcast officers, and,
> among other things, a professional repertory company.
> The Irish broadcasting service had never had it so
> good.

In 1953, the then Minister for Posts and Telegraphs,
Mr Erskine Childers, later to become fourth President of
Ireland, appointed a five-man council to be responsible
to him for the control and supervision of the broadcasting
service. It had no statutory powers but the Minister,
while retaining legal responsibility, gave it a good deal
of operating freedom. This was a big step forward but it
was still only an interim stage between civil service
control and independence.

Golden jubilee

By 1960, when the legislation to set up a television service was being proposed, radio licences had increased to
500,000, compared with less than 30,000 in 1929. But the
radio service was still under-financed. Adequate reception was not possible throughout the whole country and
there were large gaps in the daily programme schedules.

Despite the demands of establishing the television
service, a phased programme of radio development was
introduced. Hours of broadcasting were gradually extended
until, in 1968, day-long transmission from 07.30 to 23.45
was started. In 1966, VHF transmitters were provided at
the five main television transmitter stations, bringing
the national radio service to areas where medium-wave
reception was inadequate. In 1972, the radio service
moved into an extensive new centre beside the television
centre. In the same year, Radio na Gaeltachta, an Irish-
language radio service, commenced broadcasting for two to
three hours a day on MF and VHF frequencies in the Irish-
speaking districts in the north-west, west and south-west

of Ireland; in 1973, this service was extended throughout the country on VHF. In 1976, the radio service celebrated its golden jubilee and retrospective credit was heaped on it for 50 years of broadcasting.

2   TELEVISION

The first live television broadcast from Ireland had been in 1955 when a BBC outside broadcast unit transmitted an England v. Ireland boxing tournament from Dublin via Belfast and Kirk-o'-Shotts, Scotland, and on to France, Belgium and Holland via Eurovision.

Initial government thinking on the television service was similar to that before the radio service was established. In 1957, the government invited proposals from private interests to provide and operate studios and transmitters in return for a licence to operate commercial programmes for a number of years.

A Television Commission, under Mr Justice George D. Murnaghan, was set up in March 1958 and reported in May 1959. In line with its terms of reference that no charge should fall on the exchequer, its majority report recommended that the television service should be run by private enterprise under the control of a public authority - the commission had received several applications for this concession - and that separate authorities should control radio and television 'for some years to come'. In August 1959 the government rejected the recommendations and announced that it had, after all, decided to set up a state-sponsored board to run both the radio and television services without commercial participation.

A four-man advisory committee, under Eamonn Andrews, an Irishman who had become well-known in British television, was set up to prepare the new service and in April 1960 the Broadcasting Authority Act was passed. Under it, the broadcasting organisation was established as a statutory corporation, the Radio Éireann Authority, as it was known until 1966 when it became the Radio Telefís Éireann Authority. On 31 December 1961 the television service was launched.

The Marconi connection

By a happy coincidence, the organisation had been able to

secure for its new headquarters the house and grounds in a
south Dublin suburb formerly owned by the family of
Marconi's Irish mother, Annie Jameson. The inventor himself is said to have been a frequent visitor there during
the early years of his radio experiments.

Here, in 1962, the new television studios were brought
into service. A transmission network, with five main
transmitters and subsidiary transposers, was gradually
provided and by 1966 some 98 per cent of the country was
able to receive a satisfactory signal.

Chapter 3

THE LEGISLATIVE BASIS OF IRISH BROADCASTING

The 1960 Act marked a major stage in the development of broadcasting in Ireland and though it has been amended on five occasions since, most substantially by an Act passed in 1976, it remains the principal piece of broadcasting legislation to the present.

Until 1960, the national broadcasting service had been a branch of the civil service, with all the bureaucratic control and limitations on independence that this implied. By assigning to the new Authority responsibility for operating the service under its general provisions, the Act gave the broadcasting organisation a large measure of independence which, despite many vicissitudes, it has succeeded in maintaining since. On occasion, it has been heavily pressurised from many quarters, including the political parties, but this, perhaps, serves to confirm the degree of independence it has exercised in practice.

1 GENERAL PROVISIONS

With some exceptions, the Act transferred powers in relation to broadcasting from the Minister for Posts and Telegraphs to the Authority of Radio Éireann, later Radio Telefís Éireann.

The Authority was charged with the responsibility for establishing and maintaining 'a national television and sound broadcasting service' and was endowed with all such powers as are necessary for, or incidental to, that purpose (section 16). The general duty of the Authority was stated and certain obligations and restrictions in respect of programming were prescribed.

2   MINISTERIAL POWERS

The principal powers reserved to the government or to the
Minister for Posts and Telegraphs were:
the appointment, remuneration and removal from office
of members of the RTE Authority; consent to the appointment or removal of the Director-General; the licensing
of broadcasting stations; approval of periods of broadcasting and the amounts of time fixed for broadcasting
advertisements; the appointments of advisory committees; payment to the Authority of the nett receipts from
broadcasting licence fees; the making of capital advances, and the issue of certain directions in regard to
broadcast matter.

The last-mentioned provision (section 31 of the Act)
empowered the Minister to direct the Authority in writing
(1) to refrain from broadcasting any particular matter or
matter of any particular class, and (2) to allocate broadcasting time for announcements by or on behalf of any
Minister of State in connection with the functions of
that Minister.

The Authority was required to keep its financial
accounts in a form approved by the Minister and to submit
annual audited accounts and an annual report of its proceedings to the Minister for laying before each House of
the Oireachtas (Parliament) (sections 25, 26).

3   DUTIES OF AUTHORITY

Only 2 of the Act's 36 sections made specific provisions
for the Authority's responsibility in regard to programming. Section 17, stating the Authority's 'general duty
with respect to national aims', provided that:
in performing its functions, the Authority shall bear
constantly in mind the national aims of restoring the
Irish language and preserving and developing the
national culture and shall endeavour to promote those
aims.

Section 18 of the Act required the Authority to ensure
that broadcasting relating to matters of public controversy or the subject of current public debate should be
presented objectively and impartially and without any
expression of the Authority's own views.

In financial matters, the Authority was required to

conduct its affairs so as to secure that its revenue met current expenditure and made 'suitable provision' towards capital requirements (section 24).

In any circumstances, such an Act would be comparatively acceptable from the broadcasters' point of view. It gave the broadcasting Authority a great measure of autonomy, protected by legislation, and it ensured that any government directives which would affect programming had to be served on the Authority in writing. Given the particular circumstances of Ireland, still a comparatively young state, born in violence and immediately afterwards torn by civil war, with a continuing internal security threat, an unsolved problem as regards Northern Ireland, economically underdeveloped and sociologically unsettled, it was a remarkably liberal piece of legislation and, by and large, provided a sound statutory framework for the first fifteen years of the restructured broadcasting service as it entered the television age.

4   RELATIONSHIPS WITH PARLIAMENT

By Parliamentary convention, the Minister for Posts and Telegraphs does not answer Dáil or Seanad questions on the day-to-day operations of RTE, though broad aspects of the broadcasting service are subject to questioning in the Oireachtas. Opportunity for a full-scale examination of all aspects of broadcasting is provided by the annual debate on the estimates for the Department of Posts and Telegraphs. The opportunity is not always availed of; the debates are often concerned with broadcasting minutiae and with the personal programme preferences of members.

Broadcasting coverage of Parliamentary proceedings is confined to reportage, analysis programmes and interviews with Ministers, deputies and senators. Ireland is the only country in western Europe where there is, so far, no permission for live coverage of Parliament even on ceremonial occasions. On only two exceptional occasions was broadcast coverage permitted: an address to both houses by President John F. Kennedy of the USA in 1963 and the fiftieth anniversary in 1969 of the inauguration of the first Dáil Éireann.

Scope for closer parliamentary supervision is provided by a new all-party Oireachtas committee, consisting of eleven members from both houses, established in early 1977

to 'examine the reports and accounts and overall operational results of State-sponsored bodies engaged in trading or commercial activities .... and to report thereon to
both Houses of the Oireachtas and make recommendations
where appropriate.' Though RTE sought exclusion from the
operations of this body, it is one of 25 organisations to
come under its purview.

The committee has much the same powers as a court of
law to send for persons, papers and records and, subject
to the consent of the Minister for the Public Service, to
engage persons with specialist or technical knowledge to
assist it with particular enquiries.

Every report adopted by the committee will be laid before both houses of the Oireachtas and will, therefore,
be open to questions in both houses. The committee will
also have power to publish its reports, together with any
evidence given to it and any related documents it thinks
appropriate.

It is too early to say whether the operations of this
committee will conflict with RTE's understanding of its
statutory obligations under the broadcasting legislation.

Chapter 4

BROADCASTING DEVELOPMENTS, 1960-76

1 ROLE IN SOCIETY

With the establishment of the new Authority and the
launching of the television service, broadcasting began to
take on a new role in Irish society. This was due in part
to the nature of the television medium itself, with its
greater impact and its more direct intrusiveness. Partly,
too, it was due to the social changes in western society
and to the response to those changes by the BBC and ITV
whose programmes were being received off-air by many Irish
viewers. Mostly, however, it stemmed from the new freedom
and the more liberal financing which Irish broadcasting
began to experience after the passing of the 1960 Act and
the introduction of television.

Up to then, the role and function of broadcasting had
been less clearly defined but also less contentious. The
civil servants kept a tight rein on the broadcasters and
while there was fairly constant criticism of the radio
service, mainly by politicians, no serious disputes developed. Most of the difficulties stemmed from inadequate
finance.

After the launching of the television service on the
last day of 1961, it was from the programming itself and
from the evolution of broadcasting's new relationship to
the state, to government and to the different elements in
Irish society, itself going through a period of rapid and
sometimes painful adjustment, that difficulties developed.

From the outset, Church authorities, particularly on
the Roman Catholic side, were dissatisfied with some
aspects of the broadcasting treatment of religion. Irish-
language enthusiasts were - and are still - bitterly

critical of the comparatively low proportion of Irish-
language programming in the television schedules. Sporting organisations wanted better coverage of their fixtures.
Groups of all kinds sought more exposure. And in a society which is both hypercritical of others and highly sensitive to criticism of itself, Irish broadcasters inevitably found the going sometimes hard.

2   CULTURAL AIMS

Most of the difficulties arose in the two areas of programming in which the 1960 Act, as noted in the last chapter, laid down specific requirements. The Authority was
required to endeavour to promote the restoration of the
Irish language and the preservation and development of the
national culture and to present matters of controversy or
current public debate objectively and impartially and
without any expression of its own views.

    The Act's vagueness in dealing with the national aims
in regard to culture was, perhaps, unavoidable. It is
hard to define a country's culture; harder still to pre-
scribe generally acceptable methods of preserving and
developing it. This is especially so in the case of Ireland where the elements in the cultural mix are so diverse
and where, for historical reasons, manifestations of a
particular cultural strand have enjoyed political and
social dominance at different times.

    The cultural clause in the 1960 Act was written in one
such context. The state was still less than forty years
old and the ideals which had inspired its founders were
still far from complete realisation. In particular, what
were held up as the most authentic expressions of the
Irish cultural heritage - the Irish language, music,
singing and games - were seen as threatened with extinc-
tion and deserving of all the support that society,
including broadcasting, could provide.

    Organisations for the propagation of Irish culture
interpreted the legislation as requiring more broadcasting
time for programming in these areas. Other organisations,
such as the Language Freedom Movement, claimed that Irish
culture was not synonymous with Gaelic culture, that programming of the kind sought was of minority interest only
and that RTE was in breach of its obligation to be impartial in its treatment of the language question controversy.

Inevitably, broadcasting was caught in the middle, condemned by one side for what was seen as a breach of its statutory obligations, criticised by the other for pandering to a vocal minority to the disadvantage of the mass of viewers and listeners.

In its first annual report for 1960-1, the broadcasting Authority had set out
to provide a programme which as far as possible would have a distinctively Irish quality, would reflect traditional Irish values and would recognise Radio Eireann's responsibility as a public service concerned with cultural and educational matters as well as with the provision of news and entertainment.

A decade later, in 'A View of Irish Broadcasting', a pamphlet prepared in 1971 but not published until 1973, the Authority analysed (p. 13) its obligation in the field of culture as meaning, in effect,
the development of a deeper appreciation of the intrinsic value of Irish language, history and tradition, the development of a better public consciousness of national identity and the encouragement of national self-respect and understanding in a comprehensive way.

At the same time, it warned that giving a disproportionate place to such programming could run the risk of creating resentment to the objective in view: the emphasis, therefore, should be on programme quality rather than on merely providing broadcasting time.

Through the years, RTE has provided Irish-language and bilingual programmes of information, entertainment and discussion, as well as educational series for those wishing to learn, or to improve their knowledge of, Irish. While the frequency and quality of such programming on both radio and television has satisfied neither side in the controversy over cultural broadcasting, the detached observer would probably agree that RTE has played an important part in fostering the Irish language, has been a key influence in popularising Irish traditional music and has been an important cultural influence, though not in an exclusive sense, in Ireland as a whole.

3   POLITICAL PROBLEMS

It was, however, in the political field that the biggest problems arose. Ireland is one of those countries - Greece

and the Netherlands come to mind in the same context -
where even the most mundane of issues can become highly
politicised and the subject of party rivalry. To find a
way through the minefield would be difficult at any time.
It was impossible during a critical time in the country's
development and when television broadcasting was in its
first enthusiastic flush, tasting a new freedom and com-
peting against rich and highly sophisticated British
channels.

Criticism from politicians of one party or another is
a normal hazard for anyone in the public eye in Ireland.
The television broadcasters who were, to use the current
cliché, in a high-profile situation, especially in the
period when television was still a comparative novelty,
were obvious targets.

Sometimes, of course, they had themselves to blame.
Occasional programmes were insensitive, badly researched,
incomplete. Shortage of staff, of time and of facilities
was often to blame; sometimes, too, programmes did not
adequately meet the required standards of objectivity
and impartiality. But the blame often lay elsewhere -
with politicians who were over-sensitive or overbearing,
with vested interests, with persons or institutions who
relied more on influence or power than on fairness and
persuasion.

'Instrument of public policy'

The most restrictive view of RTE's status was expressed
in 1966 by the then Taoiseach (Prime Minister), Mr Seán
Lemass. He said during a Dáil discussion on a clash between a Cabinet Minister and RTE:
> Radio Telefís Éireann was set up by legislation as an
> instrument of public policy and as such is responsible
> to the government....The government reject the view
> that Radio Telefís Éireann should be, either generally
> or in regard to its current affairs and news pro-
> grammes, completely independent of government super-
> vision. It has the duty, while maintaining impartial-
> ity between political parties...to sustain public res-
> pect for the institutions of government and, where
> appropriate, to assist public understanding of the
> policies enshrined in legislation enacted by the
> Oireachtas. The government will take such action...as
> may be necessary to ensure that Radio Telefís Éireann
> does not deviate from the due performance of this duty.

It is true that no government has actually imposed, nor has RTE accepted as valid, the restrictions which this interpretation might imply.

In 'A View of Irish Broadcasting', the RTE Authority stated sharply (p. 9) that:
The preservation of the status quo is not necessarily always in the public interest: neither is the public interest necessarily always in complete harmony with every action or lack of action by government. A democratic society assumes that its broadcasting system should serve the public interest.

Friction continued to be caused by the government's concern about what it regarded as unsustainable programming, by interference and pressure from Ministers, by government opposition to a proposal to send an RTE team to North Vietnam in 1967 and later, in 1969, by the establishment of a judicial tribunal, which sat for fifty days, examined 141 witnesses and cost the taxpayers an estimated £250,000 to examine the authenticity of a television programme about illegal money-lending in Dublin.

Ministerial directions

The deroulement of the Northern Ireland situation since 1969 created further difficulties. The Northern crisis threatened to develop into a civil war into which the Republic would almost inevitably have been drawn. The authority of the government in the Republic itself was also challenged by the IRA. In such dangerous times, the government was sensitive to broadcasting coverage, which was adjudged by a subsequent Broadcasting Review Committee in 1974 not always to have conformed to an adequate standard of objectivity and impartiality.

For its part, RTE felt it had to report developments including the views, as expressed by them, of spokesmen for the Official and Provisional wings of the IRA and their respective political wings. After several such interviews the Minister for Posts and Telegraphs, Mr Gerard Collins, on 1 October 1971 directed RTE in writing under section 31 of the Broadcasting Authority Act
to refrain from broadcasting any matter that could be calculated to promote the aims and activities of any organisation which engages in, encourages or advocates the attaining of any particular objective by violent means.

In a statement following the receipt of the direction, the Authority claimed that RTE staff had conscientiously endeavoured to provide the community with a comprehensive news and current affairs service including coverage of violent events taking place in the North and elsewhere. The statement expressed the Authority's belief that it would be failing in its statutory duty were it to ignore the existence of any significant developments in the community, legal or illegal, and that in discharging its functions it did not believe that it helped to promote the aims and activities of any organisation of the type referred to in the direction. The statement concluded by saying that in spite of the added difficulty which the direction would cause, the Authority, fully conscious of all the responsibilities involved, would endeavour to provide a balanced, comprehensive and authentic service, fully responsive to the needs of the whole community.

Despite the Authority's request, the Minister for Posts and Telegraphs refused to clarify the direction, saying he was not prepared to enter into correspondence about the direction which spoke for itself.

The difficulties connected with coverage of the Northern situation continued and on three occasions in mid-1972 RTE coverage was the subject of questions in Dáil Eireann. Finally, in November 1972, RTE broadcast a reporter's summary of an interview with a Provisional IRA spokesman as part of a general survey of reaction to an important development in the Northern Ireland situation. The Minister called for an immediate meeting of the Authority to consider what action it intended to take following what he considered a contravention of his direction. The Authority, in its reply, stressed the efforts it had made to comply with what it felt was a vague direction but accepted there had been defective editorial judgment. Next day, the government dismissed the entire Authority and appointed another in its place, the Minister brushing aside the outgoing Authority's reply as 'long-winded and waffling'.

The outgoing Authority defended itself against what was widely regarded as a politically inspired action, designed to convince British opinion about the sincerity of the government's anti-IRA stance. The dismissed chairman, Mr Dónal Ó Móráin, charged that the vagueness of the ministerial direction had set the Authority an impossible task, not knowing who was to judge their performance and without a right of appeal. A university professor, Professor T.W.

Moody, Professor of Modern History, Trinity College, who
had been an Authority member, put the blame on the conflict between what the government clearly believed was a
serious matter of State security and the Authority's
belief in its obligation to report what was happening in
the country.

The affair marked the low-point of government-RTE
relations and had a sequel in legislation prepared by
a later administration, in opposition at the time of the
dismissal, providing that Authority members could be
removed from office by the government, for stated reasons,
if and only if, resolutions calling for such removal were
passed by both Houses of the Oireachtas.

Following further broadcasts which caused concern to
the government, another direction was served on the
Authority in October 1976 prohibiting the broadcast of
interviews or reports of interviews with a spokesman or
spokesmen for the Provisional IRA, Official IRA, Provisional Sinn Fein (the political wing of the Provisional
IRA) or of organisations proscribed in Northern Ireland.

With the passing of the 1976 Broadcasting Authority
(Amendment) Act, the sub-section under which the former
directions had been served was amended and the two directions automatically lapsed. On 20 January 1977 a new
direction was issued which repeated the terms of the
1976 direction.

As will be seen, all three directions were the subject
of detailed guidelines issued by the RTE Authority to its
staff providing instructions for handling material which
was - or could be held to be - covered by the directions.
In general, the guidelines listed areas where broadcast
treatment of a particular kind was prohibited or was
subject to certain restrictions and required upward reference in cases of doubt.

Despite all its problems, however, the broadcasting
service continued to make progress. Studios were built,
facilities acquired, staff recruited, programmes made.
The transmission system was extended to give total coverage throughout the country. Colour transmission was
introduced on television and stereo broadcasting on radio.
By 1976, RTE had a fully developed radio and colour television service and was ready for the next major stage in
its development, the introduction of second channels on
both media.

4   BROADCASTING REVIEW COMMITTEE

Changes in broadcasting legislation in the fifteen years
after the 1960 Act were of a minor character. In 1956 and
1972, further technical amendments were made to the Wireless Telegraphy Act, 1926, which was also amended by the
1960 Broadcasting Authority Act. The 1960 Act was itself
amended in 1964, 1966, 1971, 1973 and 1974, the amendments dealing mainly with the extension of financial provisions. The only noteworthy change in the basic legislation was the change in the name of the Authority - from
Radio Éireann Authority to Radio Telefís Éireann Authority - in 1966.

In June 1971, however, when RTE had been broadcasting
in television for 10 years, the government decided that it
was timely to review the progress of the radio and television services since 1960 and to obtain recommendations
for further development. A Broadcasting Review Committee
was set up under Mr Justice George D. Murnaghan who had
chaired the Television Commission in 1958-9.

In its final report, published in 1974, the Committee
put forward the following main recommendations:

1 Some broad definitions of the purpose and objectives
   of broadcasting should be set out explicitly in
   legislation to the following effect:
   (a) The broadcasting system should be effectively
       owned and controlled by bodies to be set up under
       this statute with responsibility for safeguard-
       ing, enriching and strengthening the cultural,
       social and economic fabric of Ireland.
   (b) The system should provide a service that is
       essentially Irish in content and character.
   (c) This service should:

       (i)   be a balanced service of information,
             enlightenment and entertainment for people
             of different ages, interests, and tastes
             covering the whole range of programming in
             fair proportion,
       (ii) be in Irish and in English, with appropriate
             provision for other languages,
       (iii) actively contribute to the flow and exchange
             of information, entertainment and culture
             within Ireland, and between Ireland and other
             countries, especially her partners in the
             European Economic Community, and

    (iv) provide for a continuing expression of Irish
         identity.

2   Broadcasting should continue to be a public service
    but the public control functions should be separated
    from the operations of the broadcasting service.   It
    proposed (a) a six- to nine-member Broadcasting Com-
    mission to supervise the broadcasting operation,
    review programme structures and performance, deal with
    complaints, etc. and (b) a Management Board consisting
    of the Director-General and the six next most senior
    executives in RTE for the day-to-day management of the
    service.

3   A second television channel should have priority; a
    second radio channel should also be provided.

4   Provision of cable or wired systems should be statut-
    orily regulated so that no one organisation would get
    a monopoly.   RTE programmes would necessarily be
    carried and private contractors should pay an annual
    contribution to RTE to offset loss of advertising
    revenue.

    In giving its reaction on the report to the Minister,
the RTE Authority welcomed the recommendations that broadcasting should continue to be a public service; that
licence fees should meet a higher proportion of RTE costs
and a higher proportion of capital investment; that current and capital financing should be planned on a three-
year basis; and that the collection of licence fees should
be undertaken by RTE.   The recommendation for the establishment of a Broadcasting Commission 'did not commend
itself' to the Authority, which said that the public
interest required a public trustee element in the body
charged with administering the resources of broadcasting.

5 TELEVISION DEVELOPMENTS

While the Broadcasting Review Committee was deliberating,
three major developments were taking place: (a) the rapid
growth of colour television transmission from the UK services and the resultant pressure on RTE to go into colour;
(b) the associated demand for high-quality wired distribution systems; and (c) the pressure for choice of television viewing in the so-called 'single-channel area',
that part of the country, containing about half the population, unable to receive UK signals 'off-air'.

(a) Colour transmission

In 1970-3, it was government policy to reduce consumer
goods imports, including colour television sets, because
of balance of payments difficulties. RTE was obliged to
limit its colour television transmissions, first to ten
hours a week and later to a gradually increasing proportion of total transmission time. The restrictions were
finally removed in July 1973 and RTE's production and
transmission were quickly converted to colour.

(b) Wired distribution

Up to 1966, wired television systems were limited to one
aerial to serve a single block of flats or a maximum of
ten adjacent homes. In that year, a major housing estate
on the outskirts of Dublin, with six 15-storey tower
blocks, was, at government request, wired by RTE for
multi-channel reception.

    In 1970, the general limit was increased to 500 con-
nections per aerial in wired distribution schemes. RTE,
recognising that this would adversely affect its advertising income, decided to engage commercially in cable
distribution and set up a special unit, RTE Relays, for
this purpose.

    RTE sought to keep a limit on the number of outlets
permitted or, alternatively, to secure a monopoly of or,
at least, first-option on, wired systems, together with
payment of royalties to RTE by private cable companies.
The government rejected the proposals and decided to give
licences to selected private companies or residents'
associations as well as to RTE for systems in areas where
off-air signals could be received.

    The Wireless Telegraphy (Wired Broadcast Relay Licence)
Regulations 1974 abolished the 500 outlets per mast maximum and provided that contractors would pay a levy of 15
per cent on gross rentals - about £2 a year per subscriber - to offset a reduction in RTE advertising income.

    At present, there are three main companies in the
Dublin area, including RTE, (with 40 per cent of the
market) and there are some 160,000 subscribers in all.
Each company provides most of the following services:
 Television: 625-line colour: RTE, BBCl, BBC2, IBA (UTV),
 IBA (Wales).

VHF Radio: RTE, Radio na Gaeltachta, BBC Radio 2, BBC
Radio 3 and BBC Radio 4.

(c) Second television channel

During the early 1970s, a major public controversy developed over the provision of a choice of television viewing
for that part of the country limited to reception of the
RTE channel. Viewers in this 'single-channel area', as it
was called, envied their countrymen in the 'multi-channel
area' who could receive two BBC services and one or two
ITV services as well. Some pressure groups were formed
to press for an extension of the UK channels to the
single-channel area via cable or microwave link. RTE, in
a submission to the Broadcasting Review Committee,
proposed instead a second national television broadcast
channel of some 24 hours a week.

In an interim report, issued in February 1973, the
Review Committee ruled out as uneconomical open re-
broadcasting of UK channels by RTE and the provision of
cable systems in the major centres of population in the
single-channel area. It recommended strongly in favour
of a second RTE broadcast channel which would carry a
selection of BBC, ITV and other foreign programmes as
well as some home-produced programming.

Meantime, the government had changed in March 1973
and in May the new Minister, Dr Conor Cruise O'Brien, put
forward a proposal for what was to be called 'an open
broadcasting area'. He told the Dáil:
    Ideally, I would like to see a much more widely effec-
    tive freedom of the airwaves over this island. I would
    like, for example, not only to have RTE programmes
    fully available in Northern Ireland, but also to have
    programmes broadcast in Northern Ireland fully avail-
    able throughout the Republic.

In October 1973, the Minister announced that the
government had authorised the provision of a transmitter
and micro-wave link network which would serve for either
re-broadcasting one Northern Ireland television channel
or for a second RTE channel.

National survey

During 1974 and the first half of 1975, the public

argument over the allocation of the second channel was at
its height. On 14 May 1975, speaking in the Seanad (upper
house), the Minister said that the government considered
that the second television network currently being
installed would be more advantageously used to re-broadcast
BBC1, Northern Ireland, that to transmit a second RTE
channel consisting mainly of a selection of British television programmes. At the same time, he acknowledged that
the case for RTE2 might not have been adequately made to
people in single-channel areas and he proposed that RTE
put on a programme or programmes describing how RTE would
use the second channel, if that were entrusted to it.

    RTE's answer was contained in a booklet, 'The Second
Channel: a statement of television development in Ireland
and the question of national choice', issued in June 1975,
in which it described the programming objectives of a two-
channel RTE service.

    In July 1975, the Minister proposed that a national
survey be held to determine the public preference on that
matter, particularly the preference of those in the single-
channel area. The Authority agreed to co-operate. The
report of the survey, published in October 1975, showed a
clear preference for RTE2 over BBC1 in both the single-
channel and multi-channel areas, the overall percentages
being 62 per cent for RTE2 and 35 per cent for BBC1. The
decisive argument was that, with the RTE2 choice, control
of the service would lie in Irish hands.

    A week later, the Minister said he accepted the results
of the survey and a statement in November confirmed that
the government had allocated the second television service
to RTE to be operated on the lines explained to those
interviewed during the survey. The network construction
went ahead but on 23 December 1976 the Minister announced
that, because of its implications for the public capital
programme for 1977 and future licence fee levels, it had
been reluctantly decided against the introduction of RTE2
in 1977. In May 1977, with a general election in the
offing, the go-ahead was given to RTE2 to come on the air
the following year.

Chapter 5

THE BROADCASTING AUTHORITY (AMENDMENT) ACT 1976

RTE's struggle for control of the second television channel had been only one of its preoccupations in the critical years between 1971 and 1976. The issue of the first
Ministerial direction in 1971, the dismissal of the Authority in 1972, the preparation of 108 memoranda on many
aspects of broadcasting to the Broadcasting Review Committee, the continued difficulties in providing comprehensive
coverage of the Northern Ireland developments, internal
changes in the organisation as it sought to strengthen its
structures, ongoing financial problems especially in the
post-1971 economic recession - all these put severe demands on the broadcasting service.

At the same time, the country itself was suffering from
the traumatic effects of the Northern troubles and economic difficulties. Government fears that a threatened
civil war in Northern Ireland would inevitably involve
the Republic and its concern about the Provisional IRA
challenge to its authority induced it in 1976 to declare
a national emergency and to force through tough law-and-
order legislation.

It was in this general atmosphere that the government
which had come into office in March 1973 introduced major
new broadcasting legislation. Inevitably coloured by the
preoccupations of the time, it proposed statutory con-
straints on the content and construction of programming of
a more detailed and elaborated nature than before, though
it also revoked the government's power to dismiss Authority members without stated reason and without Parliamentary approval.

The bill took account of some of recommendations (see
chapter 4) of the Broadcasting Review Committee which had

produced its final report in 1974. It accepted that the
legislation should state some broad description of the
purpose and objectives of the broadcasting service. It
retained the public service concept of broadcasting but it
rejected the Review Committee's recommendation for the
establishment of a Broadcasting Commission to supervise
the whole broadcasting operation. It made no specific
provision for a second television or radio service and it
did not accept the Commission's recommendations in relation to cable or wired systems.

Passed into law in December 1976, the Act contains 22
sections, 10 of which are of a technical character. One
section provides that a member of the Authority could be
dismissed only by the government, for stated reasons, and
only if resolutions calling for such removal had been
passed by both Houses of the Oireachtas. Others provide
for easier assignment of additional functions to the
Authority in respect of subsidiary activities; greater
flexibility in fixing permitted hours of broadcasting and
the incidence of advertising on radio and television; a
broadening of the Authority's financial base by specifying
the future annual amounts to be paid to it; an increase
in the limit on repayable Exchequer advances and an extension of the Authority's borrowing powers. Six sections of
special importance to broadcasters concern:
  (i) the general duty of the RTE Authority in regard to
      Irish culture, peace and understanding in Ireland
      and the formation of public awareness about the
      traditions of other countries, particularly EEC
      countries;
 (ii) objectivity and impartiality in news and current
      affairs; prohibition on the broadcasting of matter
      considered likely to incite to crime or as tending
      to undermine the authority of the State; the intru-
      sion on individual privacy;
(iii) the power of the Minister to prohibit the broad-
      casting of particular matter or matter of a parti-
      cular class which, in his opinion, would be likely
      to promote, or incite to, crime or would tend to
      undermine the authority of the State;
 (iv) the appointment of a Broadcasting Complaints Com-
      mission to deal with complaints of non-compliance
      with particular statutory requirements;
  (v) the obligation to record every broadcast in a
      manner approved by the Broadcasting Complaints Com-
      mission and to keep the recordings for at least 180
      days;
 (vi) the appointment of advisory committees and advisers.

1   GENERAL DUTY OF AUTHORITY

The main change in the 1976 Act was to restate the general
duty of the RTE Authority. The earlier Act, as has been
seen, provided that the Authority should promote the restoration of the Irish language and the preservation and
development of the national culture. The new section, in
line with the recommendations made by the Broadcasting
Review Committee, is much more wide-ranging. It provides
that:

> In performing its functions, the Authority shall in its
> programming -
> (a) be responsive to the interests and concerns of the
>   whole community, be mindful of the need for under-
>   standing and peace within the whole island of Ire-
>   land, ensure that the programmes reflect the varied
>   elements which make up the culture of the people of
>   the whole island of Ireland, and have special
>   regard for the elements which distinguish that cul-
>   ture and in particular for the Irish language;
> (b) uphold the democratic values enshrined in the Con-
>   stitution, especially those relating to rightful
>   liberty of expression; and
> (c) have regard to the need for the formation of public
>   awareness and understanding of the values and tra-
>   ditions of countries other than the State, includ-
>   ing in particular those of such countries which are
>   members of the European Economic Community.

Such generally expressed exhortations are part of
broadcasting legislation in many countries. In some res-
pects, the section in the new Irish Act, with its emphasis
on programming, is an improvement on the section in the
earlier Act. So far, no interpretation or guidelines concerning it have been issued for RTE broadcasters. It will
fall to the Authority, in its ongoing policy formation and
monitoring, to ensure that this general duty is observed.

2   OBJECTIVITY AND IMPARTIALITY

Where the earlier Act provided that broadcasts relating to
matters of public controversy or the subject of current
public debate must be presented objectively and impartially and without any expression of the Authority's own
views, the new Act sets out the following main requirements.

News

All news broadcast by the Authority must be reported and presented in an objective and impartial manner and without any expression of the Authority's own views.

The requirement of objectivity and impartiality and of non-expression of the Authority's own views is thus extended to cover all news broadcasts and not only those relating to matters of public controversy or current debate.

Current affairs

The broadcast treatment of current affairs, including matters which are either of public controversy or the subject of current public debate, must be fair to all interests concerned and the broadcast matter must be presented in an objective and impartial manner and without any expression of the Authority's own views.

This extends the scope of the statutory requirement as to objectivity and impartiality to cover all current affairs broadcasting and not just treatment of matters of public controversy or current public debate. In addition, all such current affairs broadcasts are now required to be fair to all interests concerned.

Authority's views

A sub-section provides that the Authority's views may be expressed in current affairs broadcasts relating to a proposal concerning broadcasting policy which is of public controversy or the subject of current public debate and which is being considered by the Government or the Minister.

Related broadcasts

Another sub-section provides that if it is impracticable in a single programme to comply with the requirements of the Act in regard to the broadcast treatment of current affairs, two or more related broadcasts may be considered as a whole, provided that the broadcasts are transmitted within a reasonable period.

Publication of material

A sub-section provides that when RTE publishes, distrib-
utes or sells material (whether written, aural or visual)
relating to news or current affairs, the material must be
presented in an objective and impartial manner.

Authority of the State

All of the statutory requirements set out under this section are subject to a new sub-section which has important
implications for Irish broadcasters. The sub-section prohibits the Authority from including in any of its broadcasts or in any material published, distributed or sold by
it 'anything which may reasonably be regarded as likely to
promote, or incite to, crime or as tending to undermine
the authority of the State'.

Privacy

Another new requirement is that 'the Authority shall not,
in its programmes and in the means employed to make such
programmes, unreasonably encroach on the privacy of an
individual'.

To help its broadcasters to interpret and comply with
the requirements outlined above, RTA has criculated a note
of guidance in the matter. This document sets out the
Authority's interpretation of objectivity and impartiality
and lays down some procedures (mainly upward referral) in
relation to programme treatment of matters to which the
statutory requirements might apply. In general, the document states that the statutory provisions in question
are not seen as requiring RTE to discontinue or diminish programming which holds society and public policy
and administration up to critical scrutiny or to deprive the citizen of the opportunity to exercise in
broadcasting his or her constitutional right of freedom
of expression and criticism.

As regards the prohibition against unreasonable
encroachment on the privacy of an individual, the Authority rules out the surreptitious use of recording devices
except in the most exceptional cases. Only the Director-
General can make such exception and only when the activity
to be recorded by surreptitious means is widely accepted
as gravely anti-social; where the broadcasting of the

information or event so obtained is recognised as serving
a really important public purpose which could not be
achieved by other means; where the use of the methods or
devices in question is shown to be indispensable to the
achievement of this purpose and where it does not contravene the law.

3   MINISTERIAL DIRECTIONS

The 1960 Act empowered the Minister for Posts and Telegraphs to direct the Authority in writing (a) to refrain
from broadcasting certain matter, or (b) to allocate
broadcasting time for any announcements by or on behalf
of any Minister of State in connection with the functions
of that Minister of State.

   The new legislation retains the latter provision (b)
above. As regards (a), the new section is more restrictive of the Minister's powers. His power to prohibit the
broadcast of matter is confined to 'any particular matter
or matter of a particular class' which, in his opinion,
'would be likely to promote or incite to, crime or would
tend to undermine the authority of the State'. Such an
order would have to be laid before each House of the
Oireachtas but if a resolution annulling it were passed by
both Houses within twenty-one sitting days afterwards,
it would be annulled accordingly. An order, if not annulled, would remain in force for a specified period not
exceeding twelve months, any extension having to be
approved by both Houses of the Oireachtas.

   At present, one such ministerial direction mentioned
earlier, is extant. This directs RTE to refrain from
broadcasting interviews or reports of interviews with
spokesmen for the IRA (both Provisional and Official IRA),
Provisional Sinn Fein, the political wing of the Provisional IRA, or organisations proscribed in Northern Ireland. Guidelines to broadcasting staff for the observance
of the direction have been issued in RTE. In general,
they require upward referral in dealing with matters
involved in the direction and are dealt with more fully in
chapter 6.

4   BROADCASTING COMPLAINTS COMMISSION

In the parliamentary debates preceding the passing of the
Act, the Minister said he proposed to appoint an appeals

tribunal on the lines of a Press Council, to which a citizen, a union, the government itself or the opposition could could go if they felt aggrieved about what they considered a lack of balance in broadcasting programmes.

Some 5 of a total of 15 pages in the new Act concern the appointment, functions and duties of a Broadcasting Complaints Commission, suggesting that it is intended to play an important role in public supervision of broadcasting in Ireland.

The Commission replaces the earlier Broadcasting Complaints Advisory Committee, set up by the Minister in February 1974, under the then section 21 of the principal Act (enabling him to appoint advisory committees or advisers). Its purpose was to advise the RTE Authority as to whether or not the committee considered justified specific complaints referred to it relating to alleged breaches of certain statutory requirements and codes of programme and advertising practice.

In its three years' existence, the committee dealt with fourteen complaints, mainly about alleged breaches of the requirement on RTE to be objective and impartial. Five of the complaints referred to programmes dealing with contraception, two to programmes on the Irish language and the remainder on a variety of topics. In all but two cases, the committee found that there had been no breach of the relevant legislation or RTE code of practice.

The three members of the committee - a former judge, a journalist and a freelance journalist and broadcaster - were re-appointed by the government on 31 March 1977 as members of the new Commission.

In notes for the guidance of complainants, the Commission stated that its jurisdiction is strictly confined to investigating and deciding the following limited classes of complaints.

News

Complaints that in broadcasting a specified item of news the Authority did not report and present it in an objective and impartial manner and without any expression of the Authority's own views, or failed to comply with the prohibition to broadcast anything which might reasonably be regarded as being likely to promote, or incite to, crime or as tending to undermine the authority of the State.

Current affairs

Complaints that in broadcasting a specified programme of
current affairs (including matters which are either of
public controversy or the subject of current public
debate), the Authority failed to be fair to all interests
concerned, or to present the broadcast matter in an objective and impartial manner and without any expression of
the Authority's own views, or failed to comply with the
prohibition to broadcast anything which might reasonably
be regarded as being likely to promote, or incite to,
crime or as tending to undermine the authority of the
State.

Ministerial prohibitions

Complaints that in broadcasting any specified matter the
Authority failed to comply with a ministerial order
directing the Authority to refrain from broadcasting a
particular matter, or matters of a particular class,
which in the opinion of the Minister would be likely to
promote or incite to crime or would tend to undermine
the authority of the State.

Invasion of privacy

Complaints that on a specified occasion the Authority in
a programme, or in the means employed to make such programme, unreasonably encroached on the privacy of an
individual.

Advertisements

Complaints that a specified advertisement contravened a
code drawn up by the Authority governing standards and
practice in broadcast advertising or the provisions of a
code prohibiting certain methods of advertising in broadcasting, or the broadcast, in particular circumstances,
of advertising.

Published matter

The Authority is empowered to prepare, publish and distribute such magazines, books, papers and other printed
matter as may seem to be conducive or incidental to its
objects and also, subject to the consent of the Minister,
to compile, publish, distribute, sell and exchange record·
ed aural and visual material.

Complaints may be entertained that any specified matter
which relates to news or current affairs (including matters of public controversy or current public debate), and
which was published, distributed or sold by the Authority
under the above powers, failed to present this matter in
an objective and impartial manner or included matter whi
might reasonably be regarded as likely to promote or in-
incite to crime or as tending to undermine the authority
of the State.

The Commission's rules of procedure provide that all
complaints must first be made in writing to the RTE Aut
ority, which will have thirty days to reply. If still
dissatisfied, the complainant has another thirty days t
send the complaint to the Commission, specifying the
nature of and reasons for the complaint and enclosing
copies of any correspondence with RTE.

An RTE employee will be given an opportunity to com
ment on a complaint if the Commission is satisfied tha
his interest is relevant to his employment and might b
affected by the complaint.

The Commission's consideration of complaints is in
private. Oral evidence may be taken and particulars
decisions reached are to be published as soon as pos
unless the Commission considers it inappropriate.

5   RECORDINGS

A section of the Act obliges RTE to record every br
in a manner approved by the Broadcasting Complaints
mission (sound-only recording of television program
sufficient) and keep the recordings for at least 18
providing them for the commission when required.
were made during the debate on the bill to require
retain videotapes of all television broadcasts fo
days. To RTE's relief, because of the costs invol
amendment to this effect was withdrawn.

6   ADVICE TO AUTHORITY

The Act empowers the Authority, with the consent of the
Minister, to appoint advisory committees or advisers. Up
to now, the Minister himself had the power to make such
appointments, after consultation with the Authority.
Since the Act was passed, RTE has appointed three advisory
committees for a two-year period. One deals with educational broadcasting; the second with Irish-language programming on the national networks; the third with Radio na
Gaeltachta, RTE's Irish-language radio service. The
Authority and the Director-General are required to 'have
regard to', but are not bound by, the advice given.

Changes in RTE

Since going to press, RTE, the Irish broadcasting
service, has changed its management structures
(see page 52 et seq. and Appendix 1). A Deputy
Director - General has been appointed and the
Director of Broadcasting Resources post has been
converted to a television post with overall responsibility for the two - channel services (other than
news) and for the development of programme-
making and other resources.

RTE: STRUCTURES AND PERFORMANCE

1 THE AUTHORITY

The RTE Authority which, as has been noted, is the sole body with statutory responsibility for broadcasting in Ireland, consists of 7 to 9 members, including the chairman. It is appointed by the government on terms determined by the government for a maximum five-year period with members being eligible for re-appointment. A member may resign at any time but may be removed from office by the government, for stated reasons, only if resolutions calling for such removal are passed by both Houses of the Oireachtas.

While Authority members see themselves as trustees for the public, they act in a personal capacity and not as representing specific areas of public life. Since 1973 a member of the RTE staff has served on successive Authorities.

In its 1973 paper, 'A View of Irish Broadcasting', the Authority stated 'the beliefs and concepts with which it approaches the discharge of its responsibility'. The existence of an independent national broadcasting service was, it said, in accordance with the democratic nature of Irish society and the Authority performed its most significant function as a trustee for the public in the formulation of overall programme policy.

Its responsibility is to exercise a general influence on the shape and balance of the broadcasting output and on the character of the programme service. It establishes patterns and priorities, it determines guidelines to govern the programme-making process and assesses performance ('A View of Irish Broadcasting', p. 11).

In what might be considered a somewhat moralistic
approach, the Authority went on to say that it
    regards itself as having the duty of endeavouring to
    extend the horizons, enlarge the understanding and
    widen the appreciation of the broadcasting audience.
    It accepts the role of encouraging higher standards of
    appreciation and discrimination in all fields.

2   MANAGEMENT STRUCTURES

The Authority is, however, a part-time board which meets
usually once a month. The Director-General, appointed by
the Authority with the consent of the Minister for Posts
and Telegraphs, is chief executive and editor-in-chief.
He is responsible to the Authority for all broadcast out-
output and general activities and is the interface between
the Authority and the executive as a whole.

RTE management structures have changed on several
occasions since 1960, reflecting changing priorities in
the service. At present, day-to-day responsibility is
exercised by the Director of Broadcasting Resources, who
attends meetings of the Authority with the Director-
General and deputises for him in his absence.

Under the Director of Broadcasting Resources, divisional heads are responsible for separate aspects of the
organisation's activities with the help, as appropriate,
of assistant divisional heads, group and department heads
and managers.

The policy of the organisation is to stress the primacy
of the programme-making process, with effectiveness in
programming and efficiency in support services as the
stated aims.

Three of the divisions are directly concerned with
broadcasting output - radio programmes, television programmes and news. The Controllers of Radio and Television
Programmes are responsible for the evolvement of the respective schedules and for the process by which the programmes are brought to transmission. This includes the
functions of planning, production and presentation as well
as responsibility for content.

Other divisions provide support service for the broadcasting output.

The Director of Engineering is responsible for the technical system and for the organisation, maintenance and development of buildings and technical equipment.

The Director of Personnel carries responsibility for policies and procedures relating to recruitment, training, management development, wages and salaries, working conditions, staff welfare and all negotiations with trade unions.

The Financial Controller is responsible for planning and controlling the financial activities of RTE and for developing and maintaining a management information service based on appropriate accounting and analytical techniques.

The Director of Commercial Affairs has responsibility for the sale of advertising time on radio and television, for bringing the advertising material to transmission and for RTE Relays, the separate RTE company involved in a wired distribution system.

The Director of Broadcasting Development is responsible for the preparation and production of policy documents, drafting of guidelines and inter-divisional liaison.

Separate areas of responsibility are under the control of senior executives who report to the Director of Broadcasting Resources, e.g. information and publications, external affairs and legal affairs.

Within the divisions, executive responsibility is devolved to group and department heads, managers, engineers-in-charge, etc. in charge of specific areas, with further devolution as appropriate.

Co-ordination between divisions is maintained by fortnightly meetings of divisional heads, responsible for decisions on major policy and administrative matters. Programme review and co-ordination is maintained by weekly meetings of the Programme Policy Committee, attended by relevant divisional and assistant divisional heads and other senior executives.

An organisation chart of RTE is attached as Appendix 1.

3   TRANSMISSION DATA

The Minister for Posts and Telegraphs is responsible for negotiating at international level agreed broadcast frequencies for Ireland and for the allocation and control of such frequencies.

The present utilisation of broadcasting frequencies is as follows.

Radio

There is one full-time and one part-time radio channel. The main channel is broadcast on MF from a transmitter at Tullamore, Co. Offaly, operating during daytime hours at 500 kw on 566 kHz. At night, the power is reduced to 150 kw (this arrangement is due to cease in November 1978 when the 1975 Geneva MF/LF allocations come into opera- tion). The transmission is duplicated on local MF trans- mitters at Dublin (5kw) and Cork (10kw), both operating on 1250 kHz, and on a VHF network. The VHF transmitters are co-sited with the main television transmitters.

Radio na Gaeltachta, RTE's Irish-language network, is broadcast on three low-power MF transmitters to provide coverage in the main Irish-speaking districts in Counties Donegal, Galway and Kerry. The service is duplicated on a second national VHF network to give country-wide reception.

The Tullamore MF transmitter gives daytime coverage of virtually 100 per cent of Ireland and can be received in the main centres in Britain where there is an Irish- born population of about one million. The VHF networks for the national service and the Radio na Gaeltachta service give 98 per cent coverage.

Ireland was allocated several additional frequencies at the 1975 MF/LF Geneva conference. An LF assignment (500 kw on 254 kHz), shared with Finland and Algeria, was obtained for a second national service if required. Fre- quencies for six fill-in stations to improve coverage of the existing national service and a number of assignments for future development of regional and local broadcasting were also obtained.

Television.

Television coverage is provided from 5 main stations at Kippure, Co. Wicklow; Mount Leinster, Co. Carlow; Mullaghanish, Co. Cork; Maghera, Co. Clare; and Truskmore, Co. Sligo and from 22 transposers. It is estimated that about 98 per cent of the population of the state lives within the range of RTE television transmissions, the other 2 per cent being spread over many small pockets, chiefly in mountainous areas.

RTE television transmissions may be satisfactorily received by about 14 per cent of the population of Northern Ireland. Transmissions on both channels are on a combination of VHF and UHF.

4 BROADCASTING SERVICES

The broadcasting legislation authorises the Authority, with the approval of the Minister for Posts and Telegraphs, to fix minimum and maximum totals of hours per annum of broadcasting on radio and television.

Details of output are as follows:
(i) The national radio service broadcasts from 07.30 to 23.45 hours Monday to Saturday and 08.00 to 23.45 on Sundays, with occasional extensions for special occasions. In 1975-6, the total national service output was 61.20 hours.
(ii) Radio na Gaeltachta, the Irish-language radio service, broadcasts from 18.00 to 21.20 hours every day. Its total output in 1975-6 was 13.12 hours.
(iii) The Cork local radio service broadcasts from 12.30 to 13.30 hours Monday to Friday. Its total output in 1975-6 was 287 hours.
(iv) Community radio broadcasting from a mobile studio totalled some 450 hours during 1975-6.

Television

The television service broadcasts typically from 16.00 - 24.00 hours Monday to Friday, with schools broadcasting on three weekday mornings in term time. At week-ends, transmissions begin in mid-morning and continue through until midnight or, on special occasions, beyond. In 1975-6 the total television output was 31.96 hours.

Radio na Gaeltachta

In addition to the national radio and television services,
RTE has established a separate Irish-language radio service, Radio na Gaeltachta (Radio Service for the Irish-
speaking area). This is designed mainly as a service for
the 45,000 people in the areas along the western seaboard
where Irish is still the spoken language, but it is also
broadcast throughout the country.

The service, which commenced in 1972 and which trans-
mits for some twenty-five hours a week, is seen as performing the valuable function of giving the Irish-speaking
areas, which are separated by some 120 miles, a common
identity and sense of belonging. It is also helping to
create a useful interchange between the various Irish-
language dialects which, while not very different, are
sufficiently distinctive to make understanding difficult.

The main studio centre is at Casla in Connemara, mid-
way down the west coast, with feeder studios in Co.
Donegal in the north-west and Co. Kerry in the south-west.
The initial capital requirements were provided by the
government as a grant, but the running costs of the service are met from RTE funds. The RTE Authority carries
final responsibility for the service and its 'ceannaire'
or controller of programmes reports to the controller of
radio programmes in RTE. An advisory committee, Comhairle
Radio na Gaeltachta, is appointed by RTE to represent the
public interest in regard to the service.

Cork area opt-out

RTE also provides opt-out programming on radio in the Cork
region and has broadcast experimental regional programming
on the main television transmitter in the south-west of the
the country.

Community radio

Experiments in community radio have also been in progress
since 1974. A mobile radio studio and a low-power transmitter are used and broadcasts can be received within a
radius of two to three miles. A key feature of the experiment is that RTE provides the studio and technical
staff and gives programme and production advice, but the
programming selection, production and presentation are

entirely the work of the local community.   Several broadcasting organisations have shown an interest in this
experiment.

5   SET COUNTS AND LISTENERSHIP

Between 90 per cent and 95 per cent of the estimated
786,000 homes in the state have at least one MF radio
receiver, over half being pocket transistors and other
portable sets.

   Between 70 and 75 per cent of all adults - about
1,500,000 people in all - listen to the radio at some
time each week-day.   Peak listening time is the 13.30
hours news bulletin, commanding an average audience of
half the total potential.   Other popular listening
periods are the news bulletins at 08.00, 09.00 and 18.30
hours.   Average listening is estimated at fifteen hours
a week.

   Ownership of VHF-capable radio sets is growing: the
latest market research figures (1975-6) indicate that 34
per cent of all households have one.   But only some 10
per cent make regular use of the band, the remainder
listening to RTE on MF frequencies.   RTE is conducting
a publicity compaign to encourage purchase and use of VHF
sets; as part of this campaign, community radio broadcasting is duplicated on VHF.

   Radio listening habits vary considerably between
radio-only and radio-cum-television homes.   At 18.30
hours, 9 per cent of television homes are switched to
radio; in the radio-only homes the figure is 44 per cent.
Listenership also varies widely according to the time: in
the evening, when television is available, radio listenership declines very sharply.

   Listenership to Radio na Gaeltachta averages 20 per
cent over the whole area, including districts where both
Irish and English are freely used.   In the districts where
Irish is the almost universally spoken language, listenership rises to 32 per cent of the total population on an
average evening, compared with 16 per cent for television
and 3 per cent for other radio services: of the total
broadcasting audience on a given day, Radio na Gaeltachta
holds some 63 per cent in the wholly Irish-speaking
districts against 31 per cent for television.   In the
mixed Irish- and English-speaking districts, the figures

are 25 per cent and 70 per cent respectively. Local news and Irish traditional music are the most popular form of programming.

Television set ownership has shown an average annual increase of 12 per cent from 1961 to 1977, that is from less than 100,000 sets to an estimated 655,000. At present, 83 per cent of all homes have television. Ownership is highest in the Dublin area (92 per cent) and lowest in the west coast province of Connacht (54 per cent). Homes least likely to have television are those of older, poorer people in rural areas.

About 44 per cent or 288,000 of the total number of sets is capable of receiving signals from BBC and IBA, and about one-quarter of the total sets can receive in colour. In multi-channel homes, where British stations can also be seen, RTE's audience share is about 60 per cent to 40 per cent for BBC-IBA. Average viewing is estimated at fifteen hours a week.

Tables 1 and 2 set out the relevant statistics.

Table 1 Set count (radio)

Households	000	%	Types of radio	000	%
Total	786	100	Mains	314	40
at least 1 radio	730	93	Pocket transistor	189	24
1 radio	550	70	Other portable	362	46
2 radios	149	19	VHF	249	34
3 radios	23	3	Car radio	47	6
4 radios	8	1			

Table 2 Set count and coverage (television)

Households	TV Homes	Coverage	RTE only	RET/UK
	000	000	%	000	000
Total	786	655	83	367	288
Urban	435	394	91	181	213
Rural	351	261	74	186	75

6   PROGRAMME POLICIES

The television service went on air eighteen months after the Broadcasting Authority was set up. The Authority duly took a modest pride in its achievement, though it later admitted that decisions had to be made for which more time and consideration would have been desirable.

In particular, two policy decisions which seemed desirable and necessary at the time have proved almost impossible of simultaneous achievement and have created difficulties ever since. First, it decided that it was necessary to mount a television service of such quantity and quality as to compete with the British services available 'off-air' to many Irish viewers and in order to maximise advertising revenue. Second, it aimed at achieving a ratio of at least 50-50 between home-produced and imported programming.

The first ambition has been, at least partially, realised and, while the quality of programming has been at times uneven, the quantity has been reasonably competitive on a channel-for-channel basis. Programme output was gradually increased - from 42 hours per week in the earlier years to 58 hours per week in 1976-7.

The second ambition - to transmit as much home-produced material as imported - has proved progressively more difficult.

In the earlier years, output of home material grew steadily until, in 1974-5, it reached a peak of 13.68 hours or 46 per cent of total output. But, as total transmission hours increased, as the novelty of seeing home material wore off and as more sophisticated production and presentation standards were expected, the amount and proportion decreased. By 1975-6, despite growing staff numbers and increased facilities, it had fallen to 13.04 hours, representing 41 per cent of total transmission. Imported material is made up almost entirely of British and US programmes.

In its publication, 'A View of Irish Broadcasting', published in 1973, the RTE Authority accepted (p. 4):
that the television service is at present too heavily dependent on overseas material and that an increase in home production should be sought in the years ahead which would at least produce a clear balance in favour of home output.

The Broadcasting Review Committee, in its final report, said of the broadcasting service as a whole that 'there has been, in general, a satisfactory "mix" of the three elements of education, information and entertainment' (p. 20) and of the television service in particular that it 'feels justified in concluding that, on the whole... the service is of a good standard' (p. 58).

As far as the radio service is concerned, the advent of television has significantly changed its character. Instead of being the principal medium, throughout the hours of broadcasting, it is now mainly a daytime medium, the main listenership being for news and news feature/ magazine programmes, chat shows aimed at housewives, current affairs, drama and music. Night-time radio tends to concentrate on special interest programming.

7 AUDIENCE PREFERENCES

On both radio and television, RTE's main news bulletins attract consistently large audiences. On radio, the largest audience of the day (over 40 per cent of all adults in the country) is for the main lunch-time half-hour news programme. On television, the main evening news bulletin (20 minutes) at peak viewing time attracts high audiences throughout the year.

One of the most popular radio programmes is a daily fifteen-minute drama serial reflecting life in a small town, scheduled in the lunch-time peak hour. Light music/ chat shows and light music programmes (straight or request programmes) are also popular with morning audiences. Next comes a daily magazine/current affairs type programme (mid-morning) which attracts a large, mainly female, audience.

On television, a weekly late-evening chat show with entertainment inserts has attracted massive audiences down the years. Another long-running drama serial transmitted weekly depicting life in a farming community has consistently attracted large audiences. Comedy shows, current affairs and film documentaries are also popular.

8 NEWS

A high proportion of RTE's total home production - over 13 per cent on radio and some 25 per cent on television - consist of news. There are 110 staff in the news division,

of whom 80 are journalists, and the total budget is about
17 per cent of RTE's programme expenditure.

Because there is no internal newsagency in Ireland, all
home news is gathered through RTE's own network of staff
journalists and 'stringer' correspondents. Staff journalists are stationed in London and Brussels and at Cork,
Galway and Letterkenny in the Republic and Belfast in
Northern Ireland. RTE subscribes to PA-Reuter and United
Press International news agencies and to Visnews, UPITN
and CBS film agencies. It also participates in the daily
Eurovision news exchanges.

The newsroom provides news bulletins for both radio and
television, in English and in Irish. A department within
the division provides current affairs programming on radio.
Major news bulletins on radio are carried at 08.00, 09.00,
13.30, 18.30, 20.30 (Irish language) and 22.00 hours, with
summaries and headlines at twelve other times during the
broadcasting day. On television there are major bulletins
at 18.15 and 21.00 hours, headlines at end of transmission
and a full Irish-language bulletin at 22.50 hours.

Since late 1974, RTE has broadcast a special short news
bulletin for the deaf. Newsreaders speak especially care-
fully and slowly so that lip-readers can follow what they
are saying: for those who cannot lip-read, the text is
reproduced on the lower part of the screen.

9 PROGRAMME OUTPUT

Programme scheduling on both radio and television is the
function of the respective controllers. Draft schedules,
outlining broad genres of programming rather than detailed
programme titles, are prepared some six months in advance
for television and three months in advance for radio.
These are considered at various levels - by the Authority
to ensure that they meet its general policy guidelines, by
the senior executive committees with a view to arriving at
corporate approval and, in detail, by the production facilities groupings on radio and television to ensure that
resources are adequate to meet the programme ambitions.
The timing and length of news programming is decided in
consultation with the head of news who is responsible for
the style, content and presentation of the actual bulletins.

Programme output on both radio and television is organised in specialised departments. Four of these depart-

ments - sport, agriculture, education and religious - are
common to both radio and television programmes divisions
and provide programmes on both media. Five departments -
features and current affairs, music, light entertainment,
drama and presentation - work to a controller and two
assistant controllers in radio; six departments - features
and current affairs, light entertainment, drama, Irish
language and children's programmes, purchased programmes
and presentation - work to a controller and two assistant
controllers on television.

The main programme categories are described below.

Features and current affairs

Programmes in the magazine and current affairs areas are
highly regarded in Ireland. These cover a wide range of
subjects from social, documentary and arts programmes to
political and general current affairs topics. It is in
this area of programming, particularly on television, that
problems most frequently arise with politicians and other
interest groups.

Drama

Ireland has an international renown in the field of drama
and plays and serials provide a substantial share - 6 to
7 per cent - of broadcasting time on both radio and television.

On radio, drama output includes original radio plays,
adaptations of successful stage plays and translations of
foreign-language radio and stage plays. Each week an
original play in the Irish language is broadcast. The
department maintains a permanent company of twenty-eight
actors and actresses. On both radio and television serial
plays are popular. A television serial, produced by a
two-camera outside broadcast unit and using a farm and
rural village locations, has won consistently high ratings
since 1965. This serial, besides providing dramatic
entertainment, is used to convey farming information and
to heighten awareness of social matters of relevance to
the rural community. Seasons of single plays are also
produced for television and these have included major
international dramas as well as new and existing works of
Irish dramatists. Adaptations of Irish short stories and
other literary works have also provided popular material.

Entertainment

Quiz shows and panel games are a popular form of entertainment on both radio and television in Ireland. Radio carries a regular satirical programme and comedy series and a
weekly review of entertainment trends. On television, the
Light Entertainment department produces a two-hour talk
and variety programme on Saturday evenings. This frequently deals with controversial matters and themes of
national interest and is credited with having had a major
influence in making respectable public discussion of pre-
viously 'taboo' topics.

Music

Music programmes are a staple feature of the radio schedule, providing about 40 per cent of transmission hours.
In a single television channel situation, music has been
less favoured, though operas and concerts are occasionally
broadcast.

The music department supervises and plans the activities of the RTE symphony orchestra of over 70 players, the
RTE concert orchestra of 35 players, the RTE singers, a
permanent professional choir, and a staff string quartet.
Besides their broadcasting commitments, these groups give
frequent public performances in Dublin and other Irish
centres and, occasionally, abroad. The participation by
the orchestras in opera seasons, music festivals and
public concerts is a major contribution to cultural activity in Ireland, where they are, in effect, the national
orchestras.

The department's output ranges from serious classical
music through light classical, popular operas, operetta,
musical comedy, ballet, film and dance music and modern
musicals to pop music, jazz and folk-music. Radio's light
entertainment produces several programmes consisting of
commercial discs, mixed with service information (weather,
traffic, road conditions, news headlines, sports results,
etc.) and commercial advertising. RTE participates in
several international events such as European Pop Jury,
Music Knows No Boundaries, Prix Jean Antoine, Slovene Pop
Song Festival, Nordring Radio Prize and Nordring Merry-go-
round.

Sport

Sport is popular in Ireland, especially among the male
half of the population, and is well catered for on RTE.
Because the national games of hurling and Gaelic football
are played on Sundays, while horse-racing and international
games like soccer and rugby take place on Saturdays, the
week-end coverage is extensive. One of the great draw-
backs of a single-channel situation, on both radio and
television, has been the problem of providing for those
not interested in sports during a lengthy sports programme.
On radio, the difficulty was overcome by carrying the
sports programme on the main MF transmitter which had
practically countrywide coverage and alternative programming on VHF and more localised MF transmitters. The introduction of second channels on both radio and television
removes this particular difficulty.

Agriculture

Agriculture is both the most important industry in Ireland,
contributing some 20 per cent of the gnp, and a way of
life for 22 per cent of the population. On radio, three
half-hour programmes on farming matters are broadcast
weekly. One deals mainly with the technical matters which
influence farm practice; another is mainly concerned with
new developments and techniques in farming; and the third
concentrates on the background to new developments in
agriculture. In addition, a weekday ten-minute feature
gives up-to-date information on news developments in agriculture and on livestock sales and prices.

On television, a weekly programme in prime time deals
with latest agricultural developments and techniques and
other matters of interest. While it is directed mainly to
farmers, it is regarded as useful in bringing the reali-
ties of farming to the attention of urban dwellers. Another programme provides a weekly report on livestock
prices. RTE programmes, made in the original six member-
countries of the EEC, helped to explain to Irish farmers
the opportunities and challenges of EEC membership. It
remains an important function of these programmes to keep
farmers informed of price and market trends in the Community and to explain how changes in the common agricultural
policy will affect Irish farmers and the Irish economy as
a whole.

Religious

Religious programming falls into two categories - the broadcasting of services conducted by the major denominations and discussion programmes about religious developments. The Church authorities, particularly on the Catholic side, have been happy to avail of the former especially in the interests of those ill at home or in hospital; less happy with programmes which treat of religion in a current affairs context or expose it to critical examination.

On radio, there are relays of religious services each Sunday and major feast-days; two discussion or documentary programmes a week on religious topics and a short religious talk at the beginning of the day's transmission.

On television, Church services are televised regularly and there is a weekly discussion programme. A pre-close-down religious talk is broadcast each evening.

Irish-language and children's programmes

Though RTE's Irish-language radio service, Radio na Gaeltachta, is seen as meeting a large part of its statutory obligation to 'have a special regard to' the Irish language, RTE also provides Irish-language programmes on its main radio and television channels. Language-teaching and refresher courses are regularly carried and Irish-language or bilingual Irish-English programmes in the current affairs, general interest, entertainment and natural history documentary areas are popular. On television, an Irish-language current affairs programme and a chat show occasionally feature in the 'Top Ten' TAM-ratings and a bilingual natural history series has an enthusiastic following. On radio, current affairs programmes as well as programmes of Irish traditional music provide favourite listening.

On the children's side, much of the programming is imported - the 'Sesame Street' series being particularly popular - but a home production, 'Wanderly Wagon', featuring a horse-drawn caravan with human and puppet inhabitants and some magic qualities, has run very successfully for many years.

Education

Schools broadcasts on television are aimed at post-primary
students and cover courses in physics, chemistry, mathem-
atics, biology, physical, human and economic geography,
social history and Irish and English literature. The programmes are designed to reinforce teachers' work, particularly where new curricula or new syllabuses are being
introduced, though the amount of new material produced
each year varies considerably in proportion to the financing available from the Department of Education which supervises the programming.

On the adult education and enrichment side, radio and
television programmes deal with arts and cultural matters,
leisure pursuits, science, technology and medicine and
similar contemporary themes. Film documentaries are
widely used to reflect different aspects of Irish life and
culture and to keep viewers informed about overseas developments.

Programme content on the national radio and television
services is fairly standard from year to year. A typical
analysis for the period 1 October 1975 to 30 September
1976 is given for radio as Appendix 2 and for television
as Appendix 3.

10 EDITORIAL CONTROLS

The Director-General, as has been noted, is editor-in-
chief as well as chief executive of RTE. The senior
executives in the various divisions, particularly the programme output divisions, keep in close contact with him on
matters of major programme or editorial interest.

The formal channel for liaison is the Programme Policy
Committee which meets at least once a week and more frequently if occasion demands. Ad hoc committees are con-
stituted for specific purposes such as planning general
election coverage and important State and other events.

Guidelines approved by the Authority govern programme
policy and practices in areas where specific statutory
laws or regulations apply. Divisional and departmental
heads, editors, producers and reporters are expected to be
fully informed on the content of such guidelines and to
apply the directions they lay down. In some instances,
reference to the Director-General is required; in others,

it may be considered advisable if the circumstances
warrant.

Guidelines on two major editorial areas are, at present, in force. The first set refers to the statutory
order issued by the Minister for Posts and Telegraphs on
20 January 1977 directing RTE to refrain from broadcasting
interviews or reports of interviews with members of the
Provisional IRA, Official IRA, Provisional Sinn Fein or
any organisation proscribed in Northern Ireland.

The guidelines provide for factual reportage in news
bulletins of statements on significant developments by
spokesmen for such organisations and the use of mute film
or stills at the discretion of the Head of News, but rule
out the use of sound recordings or sound-on-film in respect of them.

In programmes other than news bulletins, the Director-
General must approve the proposed programme treatment,
including any approach to the organisation in question,
before any positive step is taken in the matter. The divisional head concerned is required to ensure that the
matter proposed to be broadcast will not conflict with
the statutory order and the approval of the Director-
General must be obtained before the matter is broadcast.

In cases of doubt about their particular responsibilities in the matter, RTE staff are required to seek
instructions at the appropriate level of responsibility.

Interpretation of legislation

The second set of editorial guidelines in RTE was first
issued in 1970 but was revised in 1977 to take account of
the legislative changes introduced by the 1976 Amendment
Act.

In interpreting broadcasting's obligation to the public,
the document states that it must generally reflect the
mores and respect the values of the society in which it
operates. It cannot, therefore, be a channel for any and
all opinions, nor can it be neutral in its basic philoso-
phy and attitudes. It says that programme material should
be selected with the intention of fully informing society
and not with the intention of giving expression to the
views of the individual programme-maker.

The guidelines define the 'objectivity' and 'impartiality' which are required in the reporting and presenting of news and current affairs and the requirement to be 'fair' to all interests in current affairs programmes. The document says that the general approach to current affairs programming should be positive and no arbitrary limitation should be placed on its scope. Changes in political, economic and cultural affairs and matters of public controversy should be fully reflected. Only in exceptional circumstances and where it would be essential to establish publicly the intent of the programme to be comprehensive, impartial and fair to all significant interests involved, would programme-makers be regarded as justified in stating that someone had declined an invitation to participate in a programme.

The statutory requirement obliging RTE not to broadcast matter 'which may reasonably be regarded as being likely to promote, or incite to, crime or as tending to undermine the authority of the state' is also interpreted in the guidelines. The document says, however, that the statutory provisions are not seen as requiring RTE to discontinue or diminish programming which holds society and public policy and administration up to critical scrutiny or to deprive the citizen of the opportunity to exercise in broadcasting his or her constitutional right of freedom of expression and criticism.

A section of this document provides guidelines on the observance of the statutory prohibition on unreasonable encroachment on the privacy of an individual in programmes or in the means employed to make programmes. The document rules out the use of surreptitious recording and filming devices that would be altogether outside normal recording and filming practice, except in the most exceptional cases where compelling reasons might be advanced for suspending the general prohibition and where the means proposed to be employed would not, in the circumstances, be regarded as constituting unreasonable encroachment on privacy.

The criteria to be used in determining such cases are listed as:
   (i) The activity to be recorded by such means must be widely accepted as gravely anti-social.
  (ii) The broadcasting of the information or event so obtained must be recognised as serving a really important public purpose which could not be achieved by other means.
 (iii) The use of such methods or devices must be shown to

be indispensable to the achievement of this purpose.
(iv) Such use must not contravene the law.
 (v) The matter is so important in itself and one in which
     consistency of judgment is so vital that the prohi-
     bition on the use of such methods and devices can be
     lifted only by the personal decision of the Director-
     General, to whom the matter should be referred by the
     appropriate divisional head.

11   ADVERTISING CODE

RTE has formulated a comprehensive code of standards for
broadcast advertising. It states that the basic principle
governing the acceptance and use of broadcast advertising
is that it should be legal, decent, honest, truthful and
in accordance with accepted standards of good taste. Because of the particular qualities of radio and television,
RTE and all its advertisiers must accept a high degree of
responsibility towards the family and the community in
general, particularly with regard to the special needs of
children, community responsibility for the advancement of
education and culture, decency and decorum in production
and propriety in the presentation of advertising.

The code provides that advertising must be clearly dis-
tinguished from programme material and lays down standards for advertising matter. The list of products or services for which advertising is not permitted includes
'hard' liquor, cigarettes and cigarette tobacco, betting,
money-lending, matrimonial agencies and a wide range of
medical products, including contraceptives.

Chapter 7

FINANCING THE
BROADCASTING SERVICE

From the beginning of the radio service in 1926, it had
been government policy that broadcasting should be finan-
cially self-supporting. The same objective was set for
the television service in the principal broadcasting Act
of 1960. The Act transferred to RTE existing broadcasting
assets valued at £249,000. It also gave the service an
initial capital grant, access to repayable government
advances (now standing at a maximum of £15 million) and
borrowing and investment powers.

At present, RTE is financed for most of its capital
requirements by repayable exchequer advances (or equivalent), currently running at approximately £11 million,
and general reserves of approximately £2.5 million.
Current financing is by way of licence fees for both
television receivers and wired relay installations and by
advertising and other revenues.

The relative contribution of broadcasting's two main
income sources - licence fees and advertising - has fluc-
tuated over the years. In the 1960s, the continuous
growth in television set ownership and in advertising
resulted in a buoyancy of income which made any increase
in licence fee levels unnecessary between 1963 and 1970.
The 1970s saw black-and-white set ownership approach saturation point while imports of colour sets were discouraged, for balance of payment reasons, by Ministerial restrictions on colour transmission by RTE.

This meant that licence fees had to be increased in 1970
(to £6), 1971 (£7.50), 1973 (£9 mono, £15 colour), 1974
(£12, £20), 1976 (£16, £27) and 1977 (£18.50, £31).
During these years, however, advertising began to assume a
dominant role in providing income and at one stage was

constituting 61 per cent of all income. The RTE Authority
said in its 1974 report that it 'regrets that it still
holds the unenviable distinction of operating the public
broadcasting service with the highest dependence on advertising of all European countries'. It aimed to reduce the
proportion to a maximum of 40 per cent.

The present trend indicates that licence fee income is
assuming greater importance, especially with an accelerat-
ing change to colour receivers and licences. In 1975-6,
for the first time since the early 1960s, licence fee
income provided a higher proportion (47 per cent) than
advertising (45 per cent) of total income.

1   LICENCE FEES

The existing statutory basis for the payment to RTE of
broadcasting licence fees is section 8 of the 1976 Act.
This authorises the Minister for Posts and Telegraphs,
with the approval of the Minister for Finance, to pay to
the RTE Authority (a) an annual amount equal to the total
licence fee receipts in that year, less expenses certified
by him as incurred in the collection of the fees, in dealing with wireless interference and in meeting the expenses
of the Broadcasting Complaints Commission; and (b) an
annual amount equal to the receipts in that year from
wired broadcast relay licence fees, less costs incurred in
collecting them.

Responsibility for issuing broadcasting receiving licences and licences for wired systems, together with responsibility for the collection of and accounting for such
fees, rests with the Minister for Posts and Telegraphs.
Though he has not done so, the Minister may, by order
under the 1960 Act, authorise RTE to grant receiving licences and, on behalf of the Minister, collect fees on such
grants. The amount of the fees is determined by the Minister for Posts and Telegraphs and the Broadcasting (Receiving Licences) Regulations 1961 lay down, inter alia,
the form the actual licence is to take. In practice,
therefore, the licence charge in Ireland is the equivalent
of a state impost. The separate charge for a radio licence was abolished in 1972 and a separate supplement in
respect of colour television receivers was introduced in
1973. Licences authorise the holder to 'keep and have
possession of', at named premises, 'apparatus for wireless
telegraphy for receiving sound and visual images in
(colour and) monochrome broadcast by a broadcasting station'.

Up to 1974, the Minister fixed the level of the licence fee without reference to any outside agency. However, the RTE Authority's application for an increase in June 1975 was referred to the National Prices Commission, an advisory committee working to the Department of Industry and Commerce and responsible for recommending on price increase applications. Though its advice is not binding - and, in fact, was rejected in the case of the first RTE application it considered - its involvement in the process of determining broadcasting licence fee levels reduces the political sensitivity involved and should help to shorten the time-lag between application and decision.

The licence fee is payable to the Department of Posts and Telegraphs. In the case of old age pensioners, a monochrome licence fee is paid on their behalf by the Department of Social Welfare, the pensioner being responsible for the colour licence supplement. No surcharge is levied on the licence fee for sets used in commercial establishments, such as hotels and public houses.

Licences are obtained by way of a single annual payment and are valid for twelve months. Licence renewal dates are confined to the first day of calendar months, e.g. a licence purchased on 30 July in one year is renewable on 1 July in the following year. To ease the problem of saving the required sum, a savings stamp booklet is available. Adhesive stamps costing £0.50 may be purchased from time to time and the booklet is surrendered at the time of purchase of the licence. The amount saved (not necessarily the full purchase price of a licence) is credited and whatever is still due is payable at the time of the purchase.

There is no surcharge or fine built into the price of the licence in the event of delay in renewal. In the case of conviction for non-payment, the Wireless Telegraphy Act 1972 stipulates that offenders are liable to a fine not exceeding £50 in the case of a first offence and, in the case of a second or subsequent such offence, to a fine not exceeding £100, and also, in every case, to forfeiture of the apparatus in respect of which the offence was committed.

Wired relay licence fee

Since 1974, RTE has benefited from a licence fee, equivalent to 15 per cent of gross rentals paid by subscribers

to wired relay systems. This fee, the equivalent of about
£2 per annum per subscriber, was imposed by the Wireless
Telegraphy (Wired Broadcast Relay Licence) Regulations
1974 as a contribution towards the finances of RTE to off-
set a possible reduction in RTE advertising income as a
result of the availability of British broadcasting services on wired systems. The regulations were incorporated
into the 1976 Amendment Act which provided that RTE would
receive annually an amount equal to the total receipts in
that year in respect of wired broadcast relay licence fees
less any expenses certified by the Minister for Posts and
Telegraphs as having been incurred in collecting them.
The amount of the fee paid over to RTE in the year ended
September 1976 was over £200,000.

Cable system

RTE's involvement in cable television systems through its
subsidiary company, RTE Relays, provides another useful
source of income. In 1975-6, the company showed an operating surplus of about £140,000, accounting entirely for
RTE's overall surplus in that year during which there was
a slight loss on broadcasting activities.

2   ADVERTISING INCOME

At the time of the establishment of the radio service in
1926, Ireland was one of the few European administrations
which permitted the broadcasting of advertising matter.
The 1960 Act gave the broadcasting Authority power to
broadcast advertisements also on television.

The current legislation provides that the RTE Authority
may determine charges and conditions for the broadcast of
advertisements, though increases in charges must be
cleared through the National Prices Commission. Total
daily times for broadcasting advertisements and the maximum advertising period in any one hour are subject to the
Minister's approval. At present, 10 per cent of television transmission time, excluding schools' broadcasts,
is available for broadcasting advertisements but not more
than 7½ minutes in any one hour may be so used. Advertising on radio is not permitted on Sundays nor between 19.00
hours and 23.00 hours on weekdays and may not exceed 6
minutes in any hour. The broadcasting of advertisements
directed towards any religious or political end or in
relation to any industrial dispute is prohibited and RTE

itself prohibits, for social and health reasons, the
advertising of cigarettes and 'hard' liquor.

RTE also controls the frequency and intensiveness of
advertising breaks. On the national radio service, advertising is carried in the form of sponsored programmes,
averaging about 15 minutes and totalling 6¼ hours a week,
and 'spots' of 15, 30, 45 and 60 seconds and totalling
about 300 minutes a week on average. Television advertising is limited to 'spots' of 15, 30, 45 and 60 seconds
as well as 5-second slides with live voice-over and 7-
second filmlets with recorded sound. Approximately 80 per
cent of available time is sold, the rates for which vary
according to audience size, time of day and day of week,
averaging £125 for a 30-second 'slot' at peak time on
radio and £400 on television.

Expenditure on advertising in the main media in Ireland - television, press and radio - amounted to some £23
million in 1976. Of this, the major portion went to
print. Expenditure on advertising on television (£7.3
million) and radio (£2.1 million) represented 32 and 9.2
per cent respectively.

3   RTE PROPOSALS

Despite the statutory requirement to fund current and
capital expenditure out of revenue, RTE has been given
very limited powers of determining its revenue.

The critical decision on licence fee levels rests with
the government. Responsibility for collecting the fees
lies with the Minister for Posts and Telegraphs. Advertising rates and other charges, such as wired system rentals, must be approved by the National Prices Commission.
Bank overdrafts or other short-term borrowing to meet
operating expenditure must be approved by the Minister for
Posts and Telegraphs whose consent, together with that of
the Minister for Finance, is also necessary for the level
of the capital programme and its financing.

In its annual reports, RTE has frequently expressed the
view that its virtual impotence in determining its revenue
is inconsistent with the statutory obligation imposed on
it. It feels that, without longer term financial security, it cannot engage in confident and efficient forward
planning, especially at a time of rapid technological progress, cost inflation and urgently required broadcasting
developments.

RTE has, therefore, proposed, so far without success, changes in the method of determining licence fee levels and collecting the fees themselves. In the short term, it is pressing for the introduction of a system of paying the licence fee by instalments and is seeking the facility of dealing directly, instead of through the Department of Posts and Telegraphs, with the National Prices Commission which makes recommendations on charges for broadcasting licence fees and advertising rates.

RTE has also proposed that responsibility for the collection of the broadcasting licence fees be assigned to it, as is permitted by the principal broadcasting Act. At present, licences may be purchased at any of the 2,185 post office retail outlets throughout the country and records are held in a manual index system by the 52 district head offices.

The cost of this collection method is high by comparison with other countries, averaging 8.5 per cent in recent years. Evasion of licence fee payments is also high, the mid-1977 estimate being about 10 per cent resulting in an estimated loss of £1.5 million a year at the present licence fee level. By centralising and computerising the collection system, RTE believes both the amount of evasion by 'pirates' and the overall cost of collecting could be reduced.

4   INTERNAL CONTROLS

RTE's internal financial control mechanism is based on three main annual budgets. They are:
  (a) Operating income and expenditure budgets, which must, as a minimum show a break-even result.
  (b) Detailed capital expenditure programme for the year.
  (c) Cash budget giving sources of financing the current and capital programmes, including maximum temporary bank borrowings, if any, required during the year.

Outline operating budgets for up to five years ahead are available at any point of time. These will show anticipated licence fee and advertising revenue, indicating any increases considered to be necessary. On the expenditure side, the operating budget is calculated under three main heads: the detailed operating costs for each of 150 cost centres in the organisation; 'direct programme costs' allocated to individual programme cost centres for buying-in a defined range of goods and services necessary for programme-making (e.g. scripts, performers' fees, travel expenses, etc.); and overhead financial charges (interest on borrowings, depreciation, etc.).

Proposed programme schedule ambitions are tested against production capacity and financial feasibility and are then modified as required.

On the capital side, a rolling five-year programme of capital commitments and expenditure is maintained. The bulk of the financing for the capital development programme is provided by repayable advances from the central exchequer of the State. Advance discussions are held with the Department of Posts and Telegraphs to determine the size of the capital programme and the amount of load capital available. At present, RTE's capital indebtedness is about £11 million and it has sought to have much of this written off as foundation capital.

Cost centres in the organisation manage their own budgets with the assistance of internal guideline documents and manuals. An internal auditor oversees the operation of individual budgets.

Each cost centre and programme department is provided every four weeks with a report detailing performance against budget provision. Each heading of expense has a specific cost heading: there are over 1,000 expenditure headings to cater for all cost centres.

Quarterly reports outlining performance under both capital and operating budgets are provided for the RTE Authority. The financial records of the organisation are integrated in such a way as to meet the requirements not only of the regular management information system but also the preparation of the annual accounts in their statutorily required form for audit on behalf of the Oireachtas (Parliament) by the Comptroller and Auditor-General.

Consultants' report

RTE's operations were closely examined by consultants appointed by the National Prices Commission, an advisory body which makes recommendations to the Minister for Industry and Commerce on applications for increases in controlled prices.

The consultants, whose report was published in summary
in September 1976 and in full in May 1977 ('Radio Telefís
Éireann: Costs and Revenues') found that, by comparison
with other organisations, 'RTE is by no means inefficient'.
To make maximum use of under-utilised resources, they recommended the provision of second television and radio
channels and they pointed to the difficulty of meeting
rapidly rising costs out of an income based on advertising
income and licence fees, over which RTE could exercise
little control.

They concluded that alternative sources of revenue
should be found, the most satisfactory of which might be a
tax on the sale or rental of television sets. However, if
licence fees were to be kept down, RTE had to cut costs by
more effective budgetary controls, by reducing overtime
payments and by negotiating reduced manning levels.

5   1975-6 FINANCIAL RESULTS

The inconsistency which RTE sees between its statutory
obligation to fund both current and capital expenditure
from current revenue and its inability to control that
revenue was noted earlier. A deficit of £350,622 was
incurred in 1974-5; in 1975-6 the small overall surplus
was due entirely to trading profits on the wired television relay system, the broadcasting activities having
been run at a slight loss.

Total income in 1975-6 was £16,303,332, an increase of
26 per cent on the previous year; total expenditure was
up 22 per cent to £16,163,809. A major portion of total
RTE expenditure consists of payroll or payroll-related
(e.g. superannuation contribution) costs, the proportions
in 1974-5 and 1975-6 being 58 per cent and 56 per cent
respectively. Like most other employers in Ireland, RTE
is bound by the terms of successive national pay agreements which have been a feature of the Irish economy
since 1970. Employers must pay the agreed terms unless
they can prove inability to do so. In 1975-6, RTE pleaded
such inability to meet current pay increases, though it
did make retrospective payments after an intensive economy
campaign and as a result of unexpected buoyancy in advertising revenue.

Programme expenditure in 1975-6 went up by 21 per cent
and engineering and general expenditure by 19 per cent but
the increased spending only compensated for domestic
inflation and falling exchange rates.

Chapter 8

TECHNICAL AND SUPPORT SERVICES

The operation and maintenance of the physical resources required for the production and national distribution of radio and television programmes are the function of the engineering division.

The division is organised in five main groups:
- (i) Central Technical Services, responsible for the design, development and maintenance of radio and television studio facilities.
- (ii) Network, responsible for the design, development, maintenance and operation of all transmitters and the fixed outside facilities (i.e. provincial studios).
- (iii) Production Facilities (Television), responsible to the director of engineering for the long-term planning of television support services, for technical standards and for general administration. (In the area of day-to-day allocation and provision of facilities for television programme-making, the group is responsible to the controller of programmes (television)).
- (iv) Production Facilities, Radio, as for television.
- (v) Engineering Administration, responsible for the control of capital planning and development, computer services and the general services of the organisation.

1 RADIO FACILITIES

RTE's radio centre, which is accommodated on the same site as the television centre, has 13 studios with comprehensive facilities for presentation, talks, drama, discussions and small music groups. A large orchestral studio caters for the RTE concert orchestra and is used for other musical and variety programmes; the RTE symphony orchestra and the RTE Singers are housed in separate accommodation in Dublin.

There are two presentation studios which route all radio centre studios and regional studios and OBs to network via the switching centre. Each of the two presentation studios is equipped with compére-operated consoles.

All of the studios are equipped with switchboards for magneto-ringing on control circuits. Talkback and cue programme are also available on the control circuits. A multi-access talkback system is available between all studio control rooms, presentation control rooms, switching centre and other control points. There is also a talkback system between each production studio and the presentation studio which selects it.

The switching centre serves both the radio and television production centres and handles all audio circuits for radio and television. It contains two control positions which can be used instead of the presentation studios when these are required for maintenance.

All of the equipment in the radio centre is of an advanced design and has solid-state circuiting throughout. The complete installation can be operated in a mono or stereo mode. Compatibility has been achieved and recordings and transmissions are made with minimum switching between modes.

Outside Dublin, there are broadcasting centres at Cork, Limerick, Waterford and Galway in the Republic and in Belfast in Northern Ireland. These provide a minimum of one radio studio with associated control room and unattended, self-operated studio for live or recorded contributions.

RTE has 6 mobile radio outside broadcast units, 4 based in Dublin, 1 in Cork and 1 in Galway. In addition, it has built a mobile radio studio equipped with a radio link to the nearest network input point. This is used largely in connection with local festivals, where it provides a community radio service. RTE supplies only two technicians to operate the mobile studio: all the programmes are prepared and presented by the local community.

The RTE distribution and contribution network is

comprehensive in design and allows for inter-connection between the provincial studio areas.   The Radio na Gael-tachta network is also integrated with the total system so that its studio centres at Casla, na Doirí Beaga and Baile na nGall may be used for contributions to the national net-work.   Details of radio facilities are given in Appendix 4.

2 TELEVISION FACILITIES

The RTE television centre contains three production studios and a presentation studio; a telecine/videotape recording area; control rooms and studios for presenta-tion and technical co-ordination of Eurovision; back-up facilities for handling home-produced film material, and office accommodation for programme and news staff.   Other buildings accommodate scenery construction, storage, cen-tral library facilities, technical services and offices.

Studio 1 is the largest studio and is suitable for pro-duction of drama, light entertainment and the larger orch-estral and audience participation shows.   Studio 2 is smaller in size and is utilised for current affairs pro-grammes, children's programmes and the less ambitious entertainment programmes.   Studio 3 is used for news, sports, magazine and schools programmes.   Studio 4 is used exclusively as a presentation studio and studio 5 is used for programme linking and for contribution to Eurovision.

Film is used extensively for news, sports, current affairs, full-length drama, feature programme inserts and documentaries.   Film facilities include shooting, colour processing, printing, editing and sound dubbing.

External programme production facilities include three outside broadcast television units and fourteen staff film crews, five of whom work exclusively on news coverage. These are supplemented by eleven contract and freelance units.

The national microwave link system provides contribu-tion circuits from five terminal points throughout the country.   These are at the five main transmitter sites. One- or two-hop paths with portable links must then be established between the chosen injection point and the outside broadcast location.   It is also possible to con-nect into the microwave link system at selected repeater station points.   Details of the television facilities are given in Appendix 5.

3   PERSONNEL SERVICES

It is RTE policy, which its decentralised organisation facilitates, to delegate responsibility within the divisional structure. But common personnel policies and procedures are also necessary and these, together with collective bargaining and the handling of industrial relations, are the responsibility of the personnel division.

Under the director of personnel, four departments deal with personnel administration, training and staff development, grading and staff relations. The organisation's personnel policies and procedures are codified in a comprehensive manual to which all staff and trade unions have access.

The personnel administration department is responsible for recruitment of staff, maintenance of central personnel records and general staff welfare. RTE is statutorily required to advertise publicly for appointments to permanent posts in the organisation.

In describing the role of its staff, the RTA Authority has said:
> Programme-making is a professional activity best carried out by professionals within the framework of policy set out by the Authority and interpreted to the staff by the Director-General. The Authority seeks to appoint the best people it can find to positions in the broadcasting service. It attaches great importance to the development of a mutual understanding and a shared concern for broadcasting between itself and its staff. ('A View of Irish Broadcasting', p. 10)

Among RTE's 1,800 staff, there are more than 200 different grade descriptions. In some of these categories, RTE is the largest single employer in Ireland: in others, it is the only employer. The grading department is responsible for the operation of the job evaluation and grading systems.

The job evaluation system, developed in conjunction with the BBC and other external consultants, has been implemented in stages over the past three years and has by now been applied to some 70 per cent of the staff. It provides an integrated method of determining agreed internal pay relativities in RTE.

The staff relations department is responsible for

salary administration, for negotiations with trade unions
and for dealing with grievances and disputes. RTE employs
members of fourteen trade unions and two professional
associations, which between them represent some 90 per
cent of the staff.

Most dealings with trade unions are on an individual
basis, though on occasion negotiations are conducted with
the unions as a group. However, efforts to form a standing group of trade union representatives or an industrial
relations council, consisting of representatives of RTE
and of the unions under an independent chairman, have not
yet been successful. Some grades of staff are represented
by two or more unions and it has not been possible to
secure trade union agreement on a single union for a particular grade.

4   STAFF

RTE staff numbers have grown by 132 per cent from 786 in
1962 to some 1,820 in 1977, reflecting both increased
output on both radio and television and more sophisticated
production techniques. In the ten years to 1977, there
was a 40 per cent growth in the numbers of television
programme staff to a total of 226; 42 per cent in radio
programming (total now 270); 67 per cent in news (112)
and 31 per cent in technical and facilities staff (869).
The salary and wages bill in the same period increased
over five times - from £1.9 million in 1967 to £10 million
in 1977.

Five categories of staff are employed - permanent,
pensionable employees, numbering about 1,650; temporary
non-pensionable staff; contract staff employed on 1- or
2-year contracts; staff employed on run-of-programme
contracts, and casual, day-to-day staff. The broadcasting
legislation provided that permanent staff are recruited
through public competition.

Eighty-six per cent of the staff work in the RTE radio
and television production centres in Donnybrook, a suburb
on the south side of Dublin; the others work in offices,
studios and technical stations throughout the country.
RTE has studios in centres throughout Ireland and in Belfast, London and Brussels.

5   TRAINING COURSES

Because it is the only broadcasting service in the Republic, RTE has to provide training courses or adaptation courses for most recruits to the organisation. Of the more than 200 categories of staff employed, ranging from the traditional craft grades to the newer specialisations required by broadcasting, many newcomers require a complete training, others need only familiarisation with the specific requirements of broadcasting.

Training for radio and television broadcasting staff in the programme, facilities and technical areas is centralised in the training and staff development department, responsible to the director of personnel. Training executives take individual responsibility for planning, conducting and evaluating particular training courses, calling on specialised expertise from the relevant department in RTE or bringing in outside experts.

Facilities consist of classrooms equipped with audio-visual aids and electronic equipment, including closed-circuit television; workshops for general and electronic maintenance courses, and two studios with associated control and apparatus rooms. Professional radio and television equipment is used and there is a 12-booth language laboratory with monitoring console and audio-visual aids.

Refresher and new equipment courses are run in modules, typically in half-day sessions, to minimise interruption of normal work. But longer term (from 1 to 39 weeks) courses are conducted for new staff or for highly specialised training, e.g. radio and television producer/directors. Outside experts provide courses on advanced reading and learning techniques, management of time and related topics. RTE also provides opportunities for staff to attend courses or seminars organised by outside bodies.

Education awards are given to staff who successfully complete third-level studies outside working hours. RTE provides occasional scholarships with paid leave and free tuition for one or two staff members to take University degrees.

Production and operational/technical courses are held in appropriate locations for staff in Radio na Gaeltachta, RTE's Irish-language radio service.

RTE also conducts two or three months 'on-the-job'
courses for nominated staff of associate members of the
EBU, notably to date ASBU (Arab States' Broadcasting
Union) and URTNA (Union des Radiodiffusions et Televisions
Nationales d'Afrique).

Consultancy services

RTE has recently developed a consultancy service for the
design and installation of broadcasting studio centres
and transmission networks. This covers the complete installation from initial feasibility studies to final com-
missioning. Direct training by RTE personnel in overseas
countries is also available.

6   CENTRAL LIBRARY

RTE's central library and archives have been developed as
a multi-media centre, handling all forms of material
required in a broadcasting organisation - books, periodicals, newspaper cuttings, scripts, films, slides, still
photographs, sound and video tapes, discs, etc. A unified
system, based on the Universal Decimal Classification, has
been developed to control all forms of documentation.

By co-ordinating the cataloguing systems, RTE has been
able to secure greater staff mobility, a common classification system for different types of material and the
uniform application of conventional library techniques.
The operation of a shift system would be less economic in
a system of independent libraries.

The main function of the library is to provide
programme-makers with information and RTE sound and video
recordings. In addition, the reference section provides
a book and information service for the organisation as a
whole.

The library also operates the organisation's sound and
video tape traffic systems; issues a bi-monthly abstract-
ing and current awareness bulletin on broadcasting matters
and is the principal Irish source for the supply of programme material to broadcasting organisations in other
countries. It takes part in Irish library co-operation
and inter-lending schemes through notification of book
purchases and holdings of periodicals and by maintaining
special collections on broadcasting and broadcast engineering.

The bulk of the library's archive holdings are RTE
recordings and film, consisting of news items, stock-shot
material, music, sound effects, drama and documentaries,
selected as being either of archival importance or likely
to be re-used in programmes. The film section also includes collections of actuality film from outside sources
representing the years 1913 to 1961. The total number of
catalogue items in the library is 400,000.

The library has a staff of 38, including a chief
librarian who reports to the head of archives; 3 librarians; 9 assistant librarians and 11 library assistants.

Chapter 9

RELATIONSHIP WITH OUTSIDE BODIES AND INDIVIDUALS

By common consent, RTE plays an important role in Irish society. For several reasons, it is a 'high-profile' organisation - as a state-sponsored body, as a medium dealing in information and social comment, and as a convenient focus for the criticism which is so marked a feature of Irish social life.

As a result, RTE tends to be credited with an influence which is impossible to prove. Some politicians, clerics, academics and social commentators assign it praise or blame for the changes in habits and attitudes of mind (whether for what is considered better or worse) which have taken place in Ireland in recent years.

Whatever the truth, there is no doubt that broadcasting, and especially television, has helped to make known more widely ideas and behavioural patterns which might otherwise have penetrated more slowly into Irish society. In particular, news feature and news magazine programmes, current affairs programmes and, especially, a television late-night show combining entertainment and discussion of controversial subjects have contributed to the dissemination of views which challenged apparent - though not always real - majority attitudes. As a result, RTE has been subjected to sustained, at times trenchant, and not always undeserved criticism of its policies, its programmes and its general performance.

The problem has been intensified for RTE because its television service, operating on one channel, has had to compete against three wealthy and high-quality British channels which can be received by half the television audience. The dissatisfaction of the other half, which has had no viewing choice, was often directed against RTE, particularly when, in fulfilment of its role as a national broadcasting service, it scheduled minority, special-interest or service-type programmes. Such programmes did not please the majority RTE-only audience; the minority groups themselves felt their interests were not sufficiently catered for.

The availability of second radio and television channels will, when fully operational, ease this particular problem. But it is unlikely to reduce the close and critical attention to which the broadcasting service is treated in the press generally or the degree of public scrutiny of broadcasting policies and practices.

1   PUBLIC RELATIONS

To deal with these matters, RTE has a head of information and publications, who has overall responsibility for liaison with the public. He prepares policy statements in consultation with the Director-General or the Director of Broadcasting Resources, represents RTE in matters of public controversey and handles complaints or queries touching important aspects of organisational policy.

Information office

The information office, under the press and information executive who reports to the head of information and publications, deals with most queries and comments received by telephone and in writing. It maintains contact with the newspapers, to which it supplies programme schedules for radio and television as well as a weekly bulletin of information about forthcoming productions. It issues releases on major programmes, together with appropriate photographs, and arranges previews of RTE productions for critics and reporters. Other publicity organised by the information office includes press conferences, RTE participation in the Eurovision song contest and similar festivals, and representation.on foreign tours by the RTE symphony orchestra.

The information office staff work on a rota system so that its services are available throughout most of the hours of broadcasting. As well as supplying information to the press by release or on request, the staff record all telephoned comments about programmes. A summary of each day's comments is circulated within 24 hours to senior executives and programme departments. In this way, RTE ensures that every caller's remarks will be brought quickly to the notice of those responsible for the programme.

2   AUDIENCE RESEARCH

Audience research provides another means of keeping in touch with public opinion and programme preferences. RTE uses two methods, quantitative and qualitative.

Quantitative measurement is supplied by TAM (Television Audience Measurement, Ltd) on a weekly basis, providing estimates of the size and composition of the audience for every television programme. Ratings are given for RTE viewing in all homes and for audiences to BBC and Ulster Television (IBA) programmes in 'multi-channel areas'.

In addition to its regular weekly measurements, TAM makes general surveys of the television public each year to update basic statistics as to set-count, colour sets, etc. The service is paid for by RTE, the advertising agencies and some leading advertisers.

On the radio side, listenership surveys have been conducted almost annually since 1963. In recent years, RTE has co-operated in a national multi-media research project, which yields annual data on a wide range of mainly quantitative data not only on RTE's radio listenership but also on press, cinema and television consumption patterns.

RTE conducts its own qualitative measurements of television and radio audience reaction by weekly sampling of opinion among randomly selected panels of 500 volunteers. Each week, one or two programmes are selected for detailed examination and comments invited from panellists. The panellists also complete a weekly reaction summary report on about twelve new programmes indicating degrees of liking or dislike. From the aggregate returns, reaction indices, ranging from 0 to 100, are calculated. The panellists are changed every year.

Copies of both the TAM reports and the panel reaction are circulated widely within RTE, though they are not generally available to the public.

The audience research department also conducts studies

on basic structural population aspects and keeps in touch with research development in European broadcasting stations through membership of GEAR (Group of European Audience Researchers).

RTE supports research in the field of communications by sponsoring a lectureship in communications in the National University of Ireland. It also commissioned a report on 'Television and Irish Society' from the Centre for Mass Communications Research at the University of Leicester, England. This was designed to discover public attitudes to television, the part it plays in Irish society and the changes in Irish society and patterns of living that have accompanied the development of television.

Programme journal

RTE publishes a weekly programme journal, the 'RTE Guide'. Its journalistic staff, under a managing editor, who reports to the head of information and publications, forms a self-contained unit within the organisation. It prepares most of the feature articles on programming, the balance being commissioned from contributors either within or outside RTE.

The 'Guide' has its own photographer, graphic artists and sub-editors though the actual printing is done on contract by an external firm. With a circulation of about 100,000 copies, the 'Guide' is RTE's principal promotional outlet not only for hard programme information but also for general information about broadcasting topics. Its circulation, however, suffers from the competition of the 'Radio Times' (BBC) and the 'TV Times' (IBA) in those parts of the country, including Dublin, where the British television services can be received.

3   DEPARTMENTAL LIAISON

RTE has no direct statutory relationship with any department of state other than the Department of Posts and Telegraphs. However, close liaison is maintained with the Department of Education in relation to schools broadcasting. Until recently, the Department financed this service and determined the priorities and objectives: the function of RTE was to interpret the brief in the light of broadcasting production practices, having regard to the range of facilities available. Because of current economic pressures, financing by the Department has been suspended.

Other programme units in RTE have informal contact with relevant government departments and RTE is, of course, represented on special committees set up to plan state occasions. It also liaises with the security authorities about the provision and protection of broadcasting services in the event of an emergency. Missing person messages are broadcast on radio after confirmation through police channels. A weekly television programme, 'Garda Patrol', is designed to enlist public co-operation to help the police force deal with crime.

4   OTHER CONTACTS

Relations with Irish organisations are the responsibility of several senior executives, determined by their specific duties in RTE. Liaison with the Department of Posts and Telegraphs is maintained by the director of broadcasting resources, the director of engineering and the financial controller respectively on general, technical and financial matters. The sales division, under the director of commercial affairs, consults the Departments of Health and of Industry and Commerce in drafting its codes of advertising and advising on public welfare promotion in radio and television. The head of educational programmes and the head of agricultural programmes work in consultation with the relevant departments on the content of schools and agricultural programmes. The political editor is the immediate point of contact with parliamentarians.

The head of sport represents RTE in dealing with the organisations representing the various sports and the director of personnel liaises with AnCO, the industrial training authority, on the development of technical skills within RTE. At the time of writing, RTE's Director-General is a member of the council and the executive committee of the Irish Management Institute. The secretary of RTE is a member of the executive of CEEP-Ireland, the Irish section of the European Institute for Public Enterprise, an organisation of public service bodies in EEC countries, and represents RTE on the council of DEVCO, a body to co-ordinate development activities of Irish state-sponsored agencies in developing countries.

On-going contact with their respective churches is maintained by the broadcasting officer for Roman Catholic programmes and the co-ordinator of Protestant programmes.

These officials are members of the staff of RTE and, although they have always been ministers of religion, they are not directly subject to the authority of their respective churches in the discharge of their broadcasting functions. At the same time, since they are recruited with the collaboration of the churches and their work involves close association with church activities, the religious advisers provide a direct link with the organised churches.

5 OUTSIDE BODIES

Formal contact with institutions outside RTE, whether situated in Ireland or abroad, is primarily the concern of the head of external relations.

RTE is an active member of the European Broadcasting Union, of which it is a founder member. At the time of writing, the Director-General of RTE is a member of the EBU administrative council and chairman of a special study group on broadcasting statistics. The controller of television programmes is vice-chairman of the executive of the Television Programmes Committee; the director of legal affairs is a vice-chairman of the legal committee and chairman of a working group on cable television; the director of engineering is a member of the bureau of the technical committee. RTE executives also serve on working parties concerned with news, sports, education, drama, music and several technical subjects.

A special EBU group, drawn from RTE's programming, technical and financial departments, meets at intervals to discuss reports from EBU meetings and to determine RTE policy in the context of European broadcasting. Under EBU patronage, RTE organises the Golden Harp Festival, an annual international competition for television programmes dealing with folklore and folk music. Relations are also close with the BBC and the ITV companies. Programming and technical areas have frequent contact at every level with these neighbouring services. The assistant director of engineering represents RTE at meetings of various national and international technical and broadcasting organisations, including CCIR and the ITU.

6 INSTITUTIONAL LIAISON

A valuable connection between the broadcasters and many

cultural bodies arises from the professional interests of
RTE staff. Since broadcasting attracts the services of
persons prominent in important areas of national life, it
is common to find broadcasters playing a role in institutions and associations of various kinds. At the time of
writing, for example, the senior assistant controller of
radio programmes is chairman of the world-famous Abbey
theatre; the director of design is a member of the board
of the National College of Art; the head of information is
chairman of the executive board of the Irish School of
Ecumenics; the head of external relations is a member of
the state-sponsored Irish-language authority Bord na
Gaeilge and is a director of the language promotional
enterprise Gael-Linn. The director of music has regular
contact with the Dublin Grand Opera Society and the Wexford Festival Opera, both of which depend on the RTE
symphony orchestra to make their productions possible.

Other important contacts at home are maintained with
bodies as varied as the trade unions, television-set
renters and local authorities. Such groups are invited
to RTE and, in turn, invite RTE personnel to address
occasional meetings in Dublin and the provinces. Staff
reporters in provincial centres as well as the senior
engineers in charge of the main transmitter installations
act as RTE representatives.

RTE also participates in seminars organised by religious, educational, agricultural and other professional
bodies.

Chapter 10

EVOLUTION OF BROADCASTING IN THE FUTURE

The immediate future of the Irish broadcasting system seems fairly secure and straightforward. A Broadcasting Review Committee reported in 1974 after three years of deliberations and, judging from precedent, another is unlikely to be appointed for a decade. A major broadcasting bill was enacted at the end of 1976 and, in the normal course, it would be unusual for further legislation to be brought forward for several years to come. The statutory position of RTE and the general legislation governing it are, therefore, relatively settled.

Future developments in broadcasting are expected to be concerned with the several projects for which contingency planning is already far advanced. These, in turn, are based on judgments concerning sociological and cultural developments in Ireland. The problem of growing polarisation between Dublin and the rest of the country was referred to in the first chapter. As far as the broadcasting service is concerned, this division shows itself in a demand from provincial areas for television choice and more local radio services.

Forward planning in RTE envisages a two-stage development programme. In the first stage, from 1978 to 1981, the emphasis will be on the development of the second channels in radio and television. In the second stage, from 1981 to 1986, the emphasis is expected to be on the development of local radio.

1   TELEVISION CHOICE

The main priority is the development of a complete second television service to provide viewing choice for that half of the total population which up to 1978 could receive only one RTE channel.

In the first few years, until additional studios and other infrastructural requirements are available, the service will rely heavily on imported programming, with home-production being confined to film and OB production and whatever studio programming can be diverted from Channel 1. The ultimate aim is to have a fully complementary two-channel service, with RTE2 providing 36 hours a week, of which 8 hours would be home produced.

RTE has stated that the overriding purpose of the two-channel service is to give all viewers in the country a choice of programmes at all times. The intention is to carry at least one programme of broad popular appeal on one channel or the other at all peak viewing hours. A wide range of the best programmes available from the two British networks and from other countries will be carried. In home-produced programming, there will be a greater emphasis on regional affairs, local news and events and direct 'access' broadcasting with local involvement.

2   RADIO

A second full-time national radio channel is also a high priority. A VHF network for an additional national service already exists and the new RTE radio centre has most of the studio and production facilities required. Until VHF-set ownership and listenership improve, the intention is to duplicate this second service on MF.

The service has already commenced on a part-time basis and will be extended in stages to a full-time schedule. RTE sees such a second radio service as permitting more balanced and comprehensive programming, ensuring a better service for minorities (including adult education) and providing an outlet for further artistic and creative endeavour.

The next development - which will probably proceed simultaneously with the consolidation of second radio and television channels - is the extension of local radio. At present, this aspect of RTE activity is confined to a daily one-hour opt-out from the Cork MF transmitter. Plans are advanced for five or six additional local radio stations on MF. The first two such stations will be Radio Shannonside, serving the Limerick-Shannon region, and

Radio Dublin.   The local stations will be run by RTE.

Provincial contribution

The launching of new radio and television channels and the
local radio stations will have a spin-off effect in developing contributions from provincial centres into the
national networks.   Over the next few years, a substantial
programme for providing further radio studios in larger
towns outside Dublin is planned.   It is contemplated that
contributions from these studios will form an important
part of the schedule of the second radio network.

At a later stage, it is planned to equip the provincial
studios either with fixed cameras or with portable electronic cameras, providing both studio and location electronic origination.

Radio na Gaeltachta

Even before many of these developments are in train, the
broadcasting hours of Radio na Gaeltachta, RTE's Irish-
language radio service, will have been extended.   Several
low-power assignments of between 0.1 kw and 2 kw for possible extensions of Radio na Gaeltachta's MF network were
obtained at the 1975 Geneva MF/LF conference.

3   PROGRAMMING

Changes in programming policies and practices are likely
to concentrate on efforts to bridge the gap between the
broadcaster and the public through greater use of outside
broadcast equipment, especially the more portable equipment now available, on the development of 'access'-type
programmes, and on informality in presentation and broadcasting techniques.

RTE is anxious to remove, as far as possible, grounds
for complaints that the broadcasting service is Dublin-
oriented and out-of-touch with thinking in the rest of the
country.   There is likely to be an expansion in the provision of regional television services as well as of local
radio to reflect interests and attitudes in the different
areas outside the capital.

RTE is also likely to press for permission to broadcast

proceedings in the Oireachtas (parliament). Earlier
requests were turned down and, at the time of writing,
Ireland is the only country in the 'western world' where
at least some parliamentary proceedings are not covered
by the audio-visual media. As a start, RTE is seeking
access to record important debates and broadcast them on
radio in edited form, with live coverage on exceptional
occasions. Continuous coverage of the various political
parties' annual conferences through the VHF radio network
in recent years has developed an appreciation and awareness among politicians of how the electronic media can
help the democratic political process.

4   ENGINEERING

Engineering developments will be concentrated on extending
the contribution system. More outside broadcast units,
especially of the miniaturised kind, more studios in different provincial centres and a more extensive contribution network are being provided. The television transmission system will be improved by the introduction of
digital techniques and more sophisticated frequency planning methods to give better coverage and to release more
radio frequency spectrum space. Higher capacity links
with improved switching are being provided by the telecommunications authorities and RTE to carry extra channels
and to simplify distribution of signals.

While Ireland is a member of the European Space Agency
and hosted in 1977 a symposium on direct satellite broadcasting under the auspices of the Agency and of the
European Broadcasting Union, an Irish satellite is not
foreseen until the 1990s. Teletext reception is already
technically possible in the eastern and northern parts of
the Republic from BBC and IBA transmitters, but RTE teletext transmissions are not envisaged at present.

Cable

The provision of cabled radio and television installations
in those parts of the country where it appears to be an
economic proposition is near completion. In some parts of
the country where off-air reception of BBC and IBA programmes is not possible, local committees are trying to
organise micro-wave links and cable distribution but the
plans are not regarded as feasible at present for financial and copyright reasons. Longer term developments in

cable will be to provide to subscribers the new Irish and British radio and television channels.

5 FINANCIAL UNCERTAINTY

Developments at the end of the 1980s and in the early 1990s will depend largely on technological advances in the interim and on national policy decisions in relation to the disposition of available resources.

The rapid escalation of broadcasting costs raises questions as to how much a country like Ireland with a relatively small population can afford to spend on its radio and television services and how RTE is to be financed. Developments like satellite telecommunication and broad-band two-way communication systems and the marvels still in the inventors' minds may be beyond the financial capacity of Ireland alone.

Already, RTE's financing capacity is heavily burdened with accumulated capital debt. The 1975-6 annual accounts showed that long-term indebtedness was the equivalent of 80 per cent of total assets.

At the same time, advertising income and licence fee income are both close to saturation levels and will almost certainly reach these limits when the developments of the next five years or so are completed. The financial future beyond that is uncertain. Alternative sources of revenue are being examined, but so far no wholly acceptable methods have suggested themselves.

The Citizens for Better Broadcasting, a research and 'ginger'group, have suggested that broadcasting, like education, policing and health services, should get an annual subvention from public funds, mainly for capital investment, to achieve the maximum quality of service, with minimum government control or censorship (1976, p. 12).

Financial problems may also force changes in the press world in Ireland. It is doubtful if Dublin can continue to support three daily newspapers, two evening papers and three Sunday papers. Mergers in both the national and provincial press are a growing likelihood, especially since the cost of changing to computerised film-setting and web off-set printing is beyond the capacity of some of the weaker concerns.

6   OVERALL CONTROL

In the longer term, the question of the form of overall
RTE control may arise.   The Broadcasting Review Committee
had recommended a Broadcasting Commission: the recommendation was rejected.   As telecommunications systems develop
and become more complex, the proposal may be revived.   If
not, the method of appointing the RTE Authority may be
reconsidered.   At present, it is appointed solely by the
government and, as noted earlier, is not representative of
vocational sections of the community.

The Citizens for Better Broadcasting favour an Authority appointed directly by the Oireachtas and 'sufficiently
broadbased to represent the entire community', including
some members elected directly by the RTE trade unions and
by trade union, employer, farming, consumer and cultural
bodies in the community (1976, pp. 12-13).

Chapter 11

TOWARDS A NATIONAL COMMUNICATIONS POLICY

The point has been made earlier that, even after nearly 60 years of self-government, Ireland is still adjusting to the major sociological and structural changes consequent on or caused by independence. It is not, therefore, surprising that there is as yet no national communications policy, in the sense of agreed identification of needs, agreed determination of objectives and policies and accepted norms and targets. Such an integrated policy could be realistically prepared only in the context of overall national planning which has yet to be attempted.

The abnormal conditions in the early decades of independence made long-term planning impossible and it was not until 1958 that a 'programme of economic expansion' was launched. It achieved a 23 per cent growth in real terms between 1959 and 1964 but, because of unfavourable external circumstances, second and third plans foundered. No central planning has operated since 1972, except for the national pay agreements between employer bodies and trade unions from 1970 to date.

Central planning in Ireland has, therefore, been closely connected with economic policies and other societal needs have tended to be considered only in relation to their economic significance. Even in the case of economic development, planning reports, especially those which recommended large-scale structural changes based on a theoretical approach rather than on the pragmatic, cautious approach favoured in Ireland, have been pigeon-holed or only partially implemented.

A major report on regional physical planning, published in 1969, was shelved. A review group into the organisation of the public services, which sat from 1966 to 1969,

99

recommended a restructuring of the public service to provide it with a co-ordinated system for the planning and
management of its activities. The main reform proposed
was to separate the functions of policy-making and execu-
tion, concentrating the attention of Ministers and higher
civil servants on policy-formulation and overall direction
and control, with executive units under civil servants
responsible for carrying out settled policy. So far, the
recommendations have been adopted experimentally in five
government departments only.

Because the proposed reforms involve a new and radi-
cally different role for Ministers, a different relationship between government and parliament and a new division
of responsibilities and functions as between central,
regional and local administration, they are not likely to
proceed very quickly, though the Government elected in
June 1977 committed itself to implementing them.

Proposed transfer

Part of the reform recommended by the review group was the
transfer of government responsibility in relation to sea,
land and air transport from the Department of Transport
and Power to the Department of Posts and Telegraphs, to be
re-named the Department of Transport and Communications.
The report further recommended that responsibility for
broadcasting should be taken from that Department and
transferred to a new Department of Culture, which would
also have responsibility for such institutions as the
National Museum, the National Gallery, and the National
College of Art. In a memorandum to the Broadcasting
Review Committee, RTE opposed the recommendation because
a Ministry of National Culture would be regarded as the
equivalent of a propaganda department; because it would
separate RTE from the department responsible for the allocation of broadcasting frequencies and for telecommunications; and because it would locate the making of broadcasting policy in civil servants rather than in the broadcasting Authority. Though the June 1977 ministerial
appointments brought the Departments of Transport and
Power and of Posts and Telegraphs under the one Minister,
there is no indication that the proposal to transfer RTE
to a new Department of National Culture will be proceeded
with and the most recent legislation has confirmed RTE's
status as an independent organisation.

In the light of the recommendation, however, it is

difficult to conclude that any integrated national communication policy is being developed. Instead, any progress in this field is more likely to be determined by the press of events rather than by positive planning.

The transport and communications sub-section of the economy is certainly expected to expand step-by-step with the increase in the production of goods, particularly in manufacturing industry. In the four years to 1977, some £140 million was invested in the telephone system as part of a programme to bring it up to the best European standards. There is still a long way to go before this is achieved on a countrywide basis.

Besides the communication system expansion necessitated by increased manufacturing, a considerable increase will also be caused by the expansion of information transfer requirements.

Consensus required

It is difficult, however, to forecast what priority will be assigned to broadcasting in the development of communications as a whole in the years ahead. In a democracy, especially one with structural economic problems, the allocation of resources needs public consensus. In Ireland, where such matters of public policy tend to be more highly politicised and, therefore, more controversial than elsewhere, such consensus is sometimes hard to obtain.

In the particular case of broadcasting, the problems are not only political and financial. To a degree, there are also psychological difficulties which are reflected in a fairly common attitude at the level of the opinion-makers. This is to regard broadcasting, particularly television, as almost exclusively an entertainment medium using scarce public resources and, in the informational field, of limited value to the public interest.

Nevertheless, there are increasing signs that the value of communications, as such, is beginning to be appreciated in the key sectors of public policy. 'Open government' has become a respectable policy aim of leading political parties, though its realisation, partly because of current difficulties, is still somewhat elusive. The parliamentary debates on the Broadcasting Act of 1976 showed a much greater awareness on the part of politicians of the role of broadcasting in the life of the nation and

its independence has been confirmed. There is a long way
to go before a national communications policy can be
formulated, agreed and implemented. But the foundations
for it have been laid.

APPENDICES

RTE ORGANISATION CHART

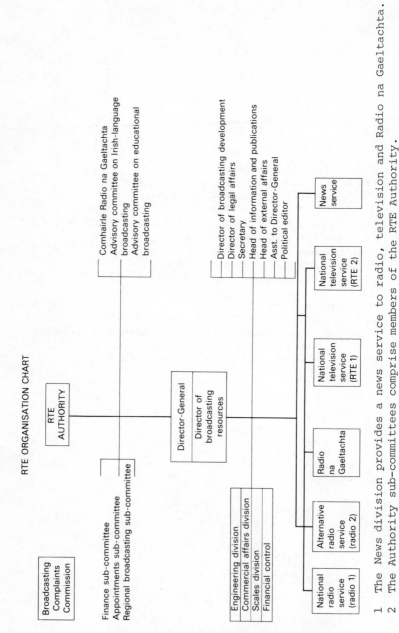

RTE ORGANISATION CHART

Broadcasting Complaints Commission

RTE AUTHORITY

Finance sub-committee
Appointments sub-committee
Regional broadcasting sub-committee

Comhairle Radio na Gaeltachta
Advisory committee on Irish-language broadcasting
Advisory committee on educational broadcasting

Director-General
Director of broadcasting resources

Engineering division
Commercial affairs division
Scales division
Financial control

Director of broadcasting development
Director of legal affairs
Secretary
Head of information and publications
Head of external affairs
Asst. to Director-General
Political editor

National radio service (radio 1)

Alternative radio service (radio 2)

Radio na Gaeltachta

National television service (RTE 1)

National television service (RTE 2)

News service

1   The News division provides a news service to radio, television and Radio na Gaeltachta.
2   The Authority sub-committees comprise members of the RTE Authority.

Appendix 2

RTE RADIO: PROGRAMME ANALYSIS
1 OCTOBER 1975 to 30 SEPTEMBER 1976

Programmes	Hours	Percentage
Sponsored	325	5.20
Talks and features	1,023	15.80
Music	2,117	39.00
Education	104	1.70
News	821	13.00
Religion	185	3.00
Sport	317	4.70
Agriculture	75	1.10
News in Irish	116	1.40
Current affairs	557	8.80
Serials & dramas	427	6.20
Variety	53	0.10
Total	6,120	100.00

Radio na Gaeltachta	1,312 hrs	
Cork Local	287 hrs	

RTE TELEVISION: PROGRAMME ANALYSIS
1 OCTOBER 1975 TO SEPTEMBER 1976

Programme	Home		Imported		Total	
	hours	%	hours	%	hours	%
1 Informational						
1.1. News	304	24			304	10
1.2. Public Affairs	76	6			76	2
1.3. Documentaries, Features	63	5	96	5	159	5
1.4. Magazines/Consumer	63	5	3		66	2
Total	506	39	99	5	605	19
2 Educational						
2.1. Schools (Syllabus)	76	6	15	1	91	3
2.2. Adult (General)	10	1	63	3	73	2
2.3. Children/Youth	21	2	100	5	121	4
2.4. Agriculture	19	2	7	-	26	1
Total	126	10	185	10	311	10
3 Entertainment						
3.1. Serious Music	4	-	14	1	18	1
3.2. Light Entertainment	189	15	304	16	493	15
3.3. Drama	35	3	214	11	249	8
3.4. Feature Films	-	-	497	26	497	16
3.5. Detective/Adventure	-	-	232	12	232	7
3.6. Sport	318	24	121	6	439	14
3.7. Children	37	3	221	12	258	8
Total	583	45	1,603	84	2,186	69

4 Religious						
4.1. Services	37	3	4	–	41	1
4.2. Other	52	4	1	–	53	2
Total	89	7	5	–	94	3

Grand total	1,304	100	1,892	100	3,196	100

IRISH LANGUAGE: TELEVISION

Programmes transmitted in the Irish language totalled 131 hours representing 10 per cent of total home production. This material can be categorised as follows:

Informational

Nuacht	58
Public affairs	15
Documentaries/nature/features	1

Educational

Schools (syllabus)	19

Entertainment

Light entertainment	29
Sport	6
Children	3
	131

Notes: (i) The form of presentation of these statistics represents the first stage in adapting to a new standarised presentation of European broadcasting statistics. Consequently, the categories might not be strictly comparable with those of previous years.
(ii) Rounding off of percentages gives rise to apparent errors in addition.

DETAILS OF RTE PRODUCTION FACILITIES,
RADIO

Of the 13 studios, 2 are used for presentation and 11 for
general production and programming.

Three of the 11 production studios, used mainly for
dubbing and editing, are equipped with a 16-channel two-
group console, three turntables, four tape recorders and
two tape cartridge players.

Each studio is also equipped with a 4-channel compere-
operated console, which can be routed to network either
directly or via its own control room console or presentation studio.

Three other studios are used for a variety of disc and
patter shows, talks and small discussion-group programmes.
They have approximately the same facilities as the first 3
studios but do not have compere-operated consoles.

Two more studios with similar facilities are larger,
discussion studios, which take in groups of ten to twenty
contributors. One of the studios has been specifically
designed for programmes with a large number of OB contributions.

There is 1 drama studio with both a 'live' and a 'dead'
room and effects mixers and 2 music studios, one of which
caters for small music groups and programmes with small
audience participation (20-40). The largest studio in the
centre accommodates the RTE light orchestra and has an
audience capacity of 140. Both of the music studios have
24-channel consoles, 16-track tape recorders and dolby
equipment.

DETAILS OF RTE PRODUCTION FACILITIES,
TELEVISION

Studio 1 (4,800 sq. ft): equipped with 3/4 Fernseh KCU
cameras with zoom lens; Thorn Q-File lighting console
(130 lamps); lit ground row and cyclorama; 26-channel Neve
sound desk with grams/tape replay; 13-channel Prowest
vision mixer with SFX and double chroma-key.

Studio 2 (2,400 sq. ft): almost similar set up, but
single chroma-key plus caption adder.

Studio 3 (540 sq. ft): 2 Fernseh KCP cameras, 60-lamp
grid, ground row and cyclorama lighting; 10-channel sound
desk and 17-channel vision mixer with SFX and chroma-key.

Studio 4 is part of a presentation area with one
Fernseh KCP camera and front projection facility, operating through an automatic vision and sound selection desk.
Vision and sound can be taken married or unmarried; 10-
channel sound desk.

Studio 5: 1 Fernseh KCP camera, fixed single lighting
position, 10-channel Chilton sound desk with grams/tape
replay, A-B-C Cox mixer with SFX and chroma-key.

Remote studios: 2 remote studios - one at Belfast and
the other in Leinster House, the parliament building - are
each equipped with one Fernseh KCP camera and linked to
the Television Centre by microwave and videocable respectively. Remote studios are being provided in several
provincial centres in the Republic.

Telecine: 4 x 16 mm. channels (3 Rank Cintel, 1 Fernseh), 3 x 35 mm. channels (Rank Cintel), 2 x 35 mm. slide
channels; all operated from central position.

VTR: 5 x 2" Quad Ampex with electronic editors, 1 x 1"
Sony U-Matic cassette machine, 2 x 1" Fernseh BCN helical-
scan machines.

Outside Broadcast units

OB2:   3/4 Fernseh KCU cameras; 16 channel Rupert Neve
       sound desk and tape replay; 6-channel Fernseh
       vision mixer with SFX

OB3:   2 Fernseh KCU cameras; 10-channel Chilton sound
       desk and tape replay; 6-channel Prowest vision
       mixer.

OB4:   2 Fernseh KCR cameras; 10-channel Rupert Neve sound
       desk; 8-channel Cox vision mixer with SFX; built-in
       AVR2 videotape recorder and built-in electrical
       generator.

VTR: 1 independent mobile Ampex VR 1200.

Links: 3 microwave associate (USA) systems, each with
       transmit and receive facilities; 2 microwave asso-
       ciate (UK) systems, each with 2 transmitters and
       receivers; 2 EMI Tx/Rec systems.

Film: News - 5 staff crews with CP16 sound cameras, plus
       1 mute camera; 3 contract crews; 13 'stringer'
       mute cameramen.
       Programmes - 8 staff crews with ACL cameras;
       6 freelance crews; 2 mute cameramen.

Editing: 16 staff editors; 4 freelance editors.

Film: Dubbing - Albrecht system with 8 replay channels;
       1 picture channel and 2 record channels. Addi-
       tional two sound studios and transfer area.

       Processing - 2 x 16 mm. Pace machines for colour
       processing (Gevachrome 700/710 and Kodak reversal
       stocks).

       Printing - 1 x 16 mm. Bell & Howell film printer.

Stills: Facilities to produce 35 mm. and 2" square colour
        transparencies.

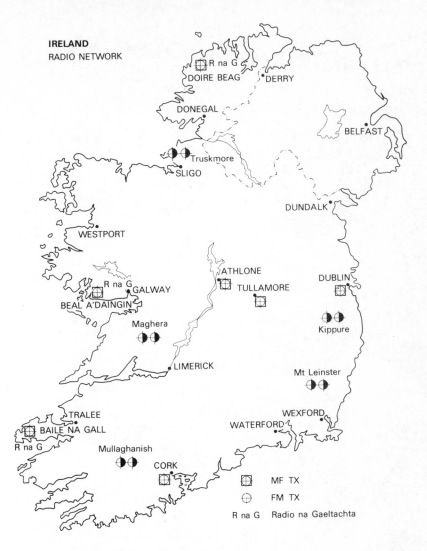

IRELAND
RADIO NETWORK

R na G
DOIRE BEAG   DERRY

DONEGAL

BELFAST

Truskmore
SLIGO

DUNDALK

WESTPORT

ATHLONE
R na G   GALWAY   TULLAMORE   DUBLIN
BEAL A'DAINGIN

Maghera   Kippure

LIMERICK

Mt Leinster

TRALEE   WEXFORD
BAILE NA GALL   WATERFORD
R na G
Mullaghanish
CORK

MF TX

FM TX

R na G   Radio na Gaeltachta

IRELAND
TELEVISION NETWORK

DERRY

DONEGAL

BELFAST

Truskmore

SLIGO

DUNDALK

WESTPORT

Cairn Hill

ATHLONE

DUBLIN

GALWAY

Three Rock

Maghera

Kippure

LIMERICK

Mt Leinster

TRALEE

WEXFORD

WATERFORD

Muliaghanish

CORK

VHF TX

UHF TX

TRANSPOSER

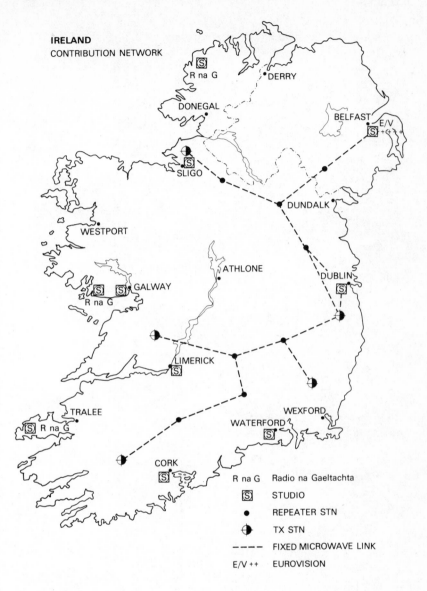

IRELAND
CONTRIBUTION NETWORK

R na G	Radio na Gaeltachta
Ⓢ	STUDIO
●	REPEATER STN
⊕	TX STN
- - - - -	FIXED MICROWAVE LINK
E/V ++	EUROVISION

RTE:SUMMARY OF FINANCIAL STATISTICS
1972-6

	12 months ended 31 Mar. '72 £	12 months ended 31 Mar. '73 £	18 months ended 30 Sept. '74 £	12 months ended 30 Sept. '75 £	12 months ended 30 Sept. '76 £
INCOME					
Licence fees	3,153,409	3,439,303	6,016,689	5,891,949	7,676,776
Advertisers					
Radio	740,864	933,357	1,710,956	1,356,686	1,770,286
Television	2,871,212	3,499,111	5,690,335	4,633,164	5,633,983
Other income	240,762	492,058	948,457	1,013,423	1,222,287
Total income	7,006,247	8,363,829	14,366,437	12,895,222	16,303,332
EXPENDITURE	6,997,016	8,096,183	14,676,165	13,245,844	16,163,809
Surplus (deficit) for year	9,231	267,646	(309,728)	(350,622)	139,523
NET VALUE OF ASSETS					
Land, buildings, plant, equipment	5,772,907	6,652,462	8,125,182	11,202,728	14,321,078
Current assets less current liabilities*	(472,096)	(381,682)	(1,742,742)	(2,913,504)	(2,332,847)
REPAYABLE ADVANCES (from Exchequer)	2,451,000	2,951,000	3,295,000	3,566,500	3,566,500
INTEREST (on Exchequer advances)	116,524	128,012	342,980	250,960	252,135
Number of employees	1,518	1,550	1,655	1,689	1,693

* ( ) indicate negative value)

Appendix 10

RTE: INCOME AND EXPENDITURE ACCOUNT
YEAR ENDED 30 SEPTEMBER 1976

	30 Sept. '76	30 Sept. '75
	£	£
INCOME		
Licence fees	7,676,776	5,891,949
Advertising - TV	5,582,959	4,593,254
- Radio	1,744,778	1,336,732
- Publications	76,532	59,864
Licence fees from cable television	207,850	152,915
Receipts from Department of Education for Educational Programmes	60,000	111,622
Other broadcasting income	203,342	141,019
RTE relays	751,095	607,867
Total	16,303,332	12,895,222
EXPENDITURE		
Programmes	9,077,522	7,514,274
Engineering & general expenditure	4,965,365	4,164,408
Remuneration & expenses of members of Authority	15,583	13,288
Bad debts written off	6,000	12,131
Interest payable	817,376	473,832
Depreciation	670,649	511,353
RTE relays	611,314	556,558
Total	16,163,809	13,245,844
APPROPRIATION ACCOUNT		
Surplus (Deficit) for the year	139,523	(350,622)
Development expenditure written off	7,567	7,567
Total	131,956	(358,189)
Surplus (deficit) brought forward from 1975	(818,167)	(511,796)
Transfer from capital reserve	-	51,818
Accumulated surplus (deficit) at 30 September 1976	(686,211)	(818,167)

115

RTE   BALANCE SHEET
AS AT 30 SEPTEMBER 1976

	30 September 1976		30 September 1975	
	£	£	£	£
Fixed assets (Schedule 4)		14,309,725		11,183,808
Development costs		11,353		18,920
CURRENT ASSETS				
Stores	448,065		450,304	
Debtors & unexpired charges	1,945,306		1,614,991	
Cash on hand	7,032		5,763	
Investments, etc.	500		500	
Total	2,400,903		2,071,558	
LESS CURRENT LIABILITIES .				
Creditors & accrued charges	3,836,904		2,817,581	
Bank overdraft	896,846		2,167,481	
Total	4,733,750		4,985,062	
Net current assets (liabilities)		(2,332,847)		(2,913,504)
Total		11,988,231		8,289,224
FINANCED AS FOLLOWS				
Value of property transferred to Authority		249,000		249,000
Repayable advances	4,000,000		4,000,000	
Less:Repaid to date	433,500	3,566,500	433,500	3,566,500
Capital reserve		736,339		798,070
General reserve	1,800,000		1,800,000	
Less: Accumulated deficit on income & expenditure A/C	686,211	1,113,789	818,167	981,833
LOANS				
Superannuation fund	600,000		600,000	
Banks	5,433,000	6,033,000	1,950,000	2,550,000
Deferred liabilities		289,603		143,821
Total		11,988,231		8,289,224

RTE: PROGRAMME EXPENDITURE
YEAR ENDED 30 SEPTEMBER 1976

	30 Sept.'76	30 Sept.'75
	£	£
TELEVISION		
Salaries & wages including		
superannuation contribution	3,877,420	3,292,945
Travelling expenses	206,108	230,659
Artistes' fees	653,726	632,578
Copyright fees	881,491	419,996
Production materials	534,226	409,178
European Broadcasting Union	110,990	68,586
Outside broadcasting facilities	42,690	45,291
Other expenses	25,498	27,968
Total	6,332,149	5,127,201
RADIO		
Salaries & wages including		
superannuation contribution	1,748,473	1,522,194
Travelling expenses	109,598	57,519
Artistes' fees	408,779	408,216
Copyright fees	104,277	119,877
Production materials	34,447	31,784
European Broadcasting Union	53,584	39,473
Outside broadcasting facilities	13,260	22,624
Other expenses	65,886	24,865
Total	2,538,304	2,226,552
RADIO NA GAELTACHTA		
Salaries & wages including		
superannuation contribution	131,310	86,855
Travelling expenses	.23,743	22,393
Artistes' fees	43,884	46,713
Production materials	2,531	1,414
Other expenses	5,601	3,146
Total	207,069	160,521
Total programme expenditure	9,077,522	7,514,274

ENGINEERING AND GENERAL EXPENDITURE
YEAR ENDED 30 SEPTEMBER 1976

	30 Sept.'76	30 Sept.'75
	£	£
TRANSMISSION & ENGINEERING SERVICES		
Salaries & wages including superannuation contribution	1,660,594	1,280,908
Travelling expenses	130,118	138,350
Lines network	337,563	208,391
Power	245,786	192,465
Maintenance of equipment	178,773	198,562
Other expenses	19,702	24,948
Total	2,572,536	2,043,624
SALES & PROMOTION		
Salaries & wages including superannuation contribution	285,540	249,392
Travelling expenses	10,197	9,812
Other expenses	105,897	97,794
Total	401,634	356,998
CENTRAL SERVICES		
Salaries & wages including superannuation contribution	1,107,872	1,010,217
Travelling expenses	48,688	37,922
Printing, postage & stationery	119,866	122,449
Telephones and Telex	147,125	103,592
Other expenses	168,570	153,739
Total	1,592,121	1,427,919
PREMISES CHARGES		
Rent, rates & insurance	244,396	223,435
Lighting, heating, cleaning & security	106,919	77,845
Maintenance of grounds & premises	47,759	34,587
Total	399,074	335,867
Total expenditure	4,965,365	4,164,408

BIBLIOGRAPHY

'Administration Yearbook and Diary' (annual), Dublin,
Institute of Public Administration.
'A View of Irish Broadcasting' (1973), RTE Authority,
Dublin, RTE.
BECKETT, J.C. (1966), 'The Making of Modern Ireland',
London, Faber.
Broadcasting Authority Act, 1960
Broadcasting Authority (Amendment) Acts, 1964/66/68/71/73/76
Broadcasting Review Committee Report, Dublin, Stationery
Office.
'Bunreacht na hEireann' (Constitution of Ireland) (1937),
Dublin Stationery Office.
'Census of Population 1971', Dublin, Stationery Office.
CHUBB, BASIL (1970), 'The Government and Politics of Ire-
land', London, OUP.
'Communications Directory and Yearbook, 1977', Dublin,
Mount Salus Press.
CULLEN, L.M. (1969), 'The Formation of the Irish Economy',
Cork, Mercier Press.
'Encyclopaedia of Ireland' (1968), Dublin, Allen Figgis.
'Facts about Ireland' (1969, 2nd edition), Dublin,
Department of Foreign Affairs.
GORHAM, MAURICE (1967), 'Forty Years of Irish Broadcast-
ing', Dublin, Talbot Press.
'Irish Statistical Bulletin' (Quarterly) Dublin, Station-
ery Office.
LYONS, F.S.L. (1971), 'Ireland since the Famine', London,
Weidenfeld & Nicholson.
MCLUHAN, MARSHALL (1964), 'Understanding Media', London,
Routledge & Kegan Paul.
MEEHAN, JAMES (1970), 'The Irish Economy since 1932',
Liverpool University Press.
O'BRIEN, CONOR CRUISE (1972), 'States of Ireland', London,
Hutchinson.

'Population and Employment Projections: 1971-86', National Economic & Social Council, Dublin, Stationery Office.
'Prelude to Planning', National Economic & Social Council, Dublin, Stationery Office.
'Radio Telefis Eireann: Costs and Revenues' (1977), National Prices Commission Occasional Paper No. 23, Dublin, Stationery Office.
'Statistical Abstract 1972-3', Dublin, Stationery Office.
THE CITIZENS FOR BETTER BROADCASTING (1976), 'Aspects of RTE Television Broadcasting', Dublin
'The Second Channel' (1975), RTE Authority, Dublin, RTE
WHITE, JACK (1975), 'Minority Report: The Protestant Community in the Irish Republic', Dublin, Gill & Macmillan.
Wireless Telegraphy Act, 1926